The
BOOK OF
INVASIVE
SPECIES

THE BOOK OF INVASIVE SPECIES

13-Digit ISBN: 978-1-64643-363-6
10-Digit ISBN: 1-64643-363-7

This book may be ordered by mail from the publisher. Please include $5.99 for postage and handling. Please support your local bookseller first!

Books published by Cider Mill Press Book Publishers are available at special discounts for bulk purchases in the United States by corporations, institutions, and other organizations. For more information, please contact the publisher.

Cider Mill Press Book Publishers
"Where good books are ready for press"
501 Nelson Place
Nashville, Tennessee 37214

cidermillpress.com

Typography: Calder, Warnock Pro

Printed in Malaysia

All vectors used under official license from Shutterstock.com.

23 24 25 26 27 OFF 5 4 3 2 1
First Edition

The BOOK OF INVASIVE SPECIES

100 Plants, Animals, and Microbes
THAT MADE THEMSELVES AT HOME

Kit Carlson, PhD, and Aaron Carlson

ILLUSTRATIONS BY EMILY SULLIVAN

CIDER MILL PRESS

BOOK PUBLISHERS

AUTHOR BIOS

DR. KIT CARLSON earned her PhD in plant microbiology and pathology at the University of Missouri, and conducted her postdoctoral research at Virginia Tech, focused on molecular diagnostics of plant disease. Kit has been a botany professor for nearly two decades. During her tenure, she has served thousands of students and developed and instructed more than 15 different plant science courses. She and her students have conducted and published research on a wide range of topics, including plant disease, medicinal plants, ethnobotany, public land, science education, and more. She is also the author of *The Book of Killer Plants* and coauthor of *Foraging: A Guide to Edible Wild Plants*.

AARON CARLSON is an award-winning naturalist recognized for his contributions to observing rare plant species in their native habitats. Aaron received his BS in Biology and Wildlife at the University of Wisconsin-Stevens Point, and attended the University of Missouri for his graduate work in limnology. When not working as an educator or lab technician, Aaron spends his free time observing and documenting the life histories of lichens, plants, fungi, and animals. Aaron lives in southern Wisconsin with his wife, two children, and their poodle. He is also the coauthor of *Foraging: A Guide to Edible Wild Plants*.

ABOUT CIDER MILL PRESS BOOK PUBLISHERS

Good ideas ripen with time. From seed to harvest, Cider Mill Press brings fine reading, information, and entertainment together between the covers of its creatively crafted books. Our Cider Mill bears fruit twice a year, publishing a new crop of titles each spring and fall.

"Where Good Books Are Ready for Press"

501 Nelson Place
Nashville, Tennessee 37214

cidermillpress.com

CONTENTS

INTRODUCTION 6

ANIMALS 15

    INVERTEBRATES 15

    FISH 59

    AMPHIBIANS 73

    REPTILES 79

    BIRDS 89

    MAMMALS 93

PLANTS 103

MICROORGANISMS 181

    BACTERIA 181

    FUNGI 189

    VIRUSES 213

OTHERS 231

GLOSSARY 236

INTRODUCTION

What do the following species have in common?

Raccoon (*Procyon lotor*), black cherry (*Prunus serotina*), largemouth bass (*Micropterus salmoides*).

If you don't know, and the title of this book didn't give you a hint, they are all common organisms native to North America that have become highly invasive in *other* parts of the world!

What exactly is an "invasive species"? The term applies to any species thriving in an area outside its natural range of dispersal, creating adverse ecological and/or economic effects in that area. Invasive species are among the greatest threats to biodiversity and one of the leading causes of species extinction—second only to habitat destruction. This book is intended to serve as a reference guide to 100 invasive species you may encounter in North America. There are many more invasive species than the ones highlighted in this guide. These species were selected because of their high potential to harm the environment, the economy, or even human health and safety.

Some claim humans are the first invasive species. Since leaving Africa 60,000 years ago, humans have colonized every part of the globe, and during this process, they have caused extinctions, spread disease, and altered landscapes in irredeemable ways. Before global human colonization, only by sheer chance would an individual organism get transported to a location outside of its native range, where it would be unlikely to survive, let alone thrive, reproduce, and spread across the new landscape. Species in the environment coevolve over eons, resulting in a complex and fascinating variety of adaptations and interactions between species and their environment. This coexistence dictates that each species becomes reliant on other species to survive and thrive. The ability to colonize new habitats was governed by the species' dispersal mechanisms and environment.

As *Homo sapiens* migrated into uncolonized ecosystems, they transported a variety of organisms into new locations. Insect eggs, larvae, and other propagules (spores, plant seeds, cuttings, etc.), including disease-causing organisms, would have traveled along in hair and clothes. Eventually, as *Homo sapiens* dispersed far and wide and settled in new lands populated by organisms unknown to them, they intentionally brought other species with them for food or cultural reasons. They also brought some species with them unintentionally; for example, the evolutionary history of invasive body lice almost mirrors the evolutionary history of primates. As humans colonized the globe, the human body louse came along for the ride and is now globally distributed. A body louse infestation causes discomfort and inconvenience. Still, some lice can harbor deadly microbial pathogens, including *Rickettsia prowazekii*, the bacteria that causes epidemic typhus—which has caused more deaths than all the wars in history.

It did not take long for many exotic species to be dispersed worldwide, affecting the yields of crops, causing the extinction of native species, and resulting in many other negative impacts. In the United States alone, there are over 6,500 species that are considered non-native and established. These species are the focus of this book. While each invasive species is unique in how and why it was introduced into an ecosystem and in the qualities that caused it to become invasive, there are specific characteristics that seem to increase the likelihood of a species becoming invasive. One characteristic is a rapid reproduction rate that allows the organism to quickly reach its reproductive stage and produce numerous offspring in a short time. A large number of offspring increases the likelihood of there being individual organisms that can survive in new ecosystems.

Another characteristic is adaptability. A species that can tolerate a broad range of environmental conditions is more likely to survive than a species with a narrower tolerance range. Tolerance also applies to the need for food and shelter. Organisms that can adapt to using various food and shelter resources are more likely to survive. The third characteristic is the absence of environmental control in the new land. The ecological interactions that evolve in native ecosystems tend to keep the population of each species in check, never allowing one species to become too dominant, usually through predator-prey relationships. If these controls do not exist in the new land, a species is more likely to survive and thrive.

Lastly, species that benefit from human activities are more likely to become invasive. The beneficial activity may involve dispersing seeds or spores, creating food or habitats, or suppressing constraints (predation, etc.) on the species.

Not all invasive species have all of these characteristics, and having all of these characteristics does not necessarily mean a species will become invasive. The habitat also plays a significant role in whether a species becomes invasive. Every habitat on Earth has a unique combination of physical, chemical, and biological characteristics that determine how sensitive a habitat is to an invasive species. This quality is known as its invasibility. Factors influencing habitat invasibility include food, water, and light availability, the amount and type of disturbance (floods, fires, etc.), and species biodiversity. Areas with high biodiversity are generally less susceptible to invasive species than areas with low biodiversity, simply due to an increased likelihood of some ecological constraint on the invasive species, such as the presence or absence of a predatory species. High biodiversity also means that a successful invasive species tends to result in lower biodiversity in the ecosystem, thus making that habitat even more vulnerable to further invasions.

Invasive species can fall into three broad categories:

1. **Those intentionally imported and released into the wild.**

Species may be intentionally imported and released for various reasons, sometimes even in an attempt to control another invasive species. For example, in 1906, a parasitic fly, *Compsilura concinnata*, was introduced into North America to control the invasive Spongy Moth, *Lymantria dispar*. It resulted in almost no reduction in Spongy Moth populations but did reduce populations of over 200 native insect species. In addition to biocontrol agents, species may be introduced to improve soil conditions or minimize erosion, to serve as game for hunting or fishing, as sources of new germplasm for breeding programs or other agricultural applications, or as ornamentals used in the landscape. It is often difficult or impossible to predict what an introduced organism will do in a new landscape. Despite the reported adverse outcomes, in some cases, introduced species have been invaluable tools in mitigating complex ecological problems. It is estimated that in scenarios in which species were deployed using careful analysis, consistent monitoring, and a science-based approach, there was almost no negative impact on native species.

2. **Those intentionally imported but which escaped from intended confinement.**

A less common pathway for new invasive species involves organisms intentionally imported but intended to be maintained in captivity. Examples usually include animals and plants imported for zoos and botanical gardens or used in the fur or meat industries. One of the most dangerous invasive species in this category is the Africanized Honeybee, *Apis mellifera* spp. *scutellata*, described later in this book.

3. Fully unintentional introductions.

Most invasive species are introduced unintentionally through negligence or ignorance or by accident. For example, many aquatic invasive species and some invasive land plant species were introduced through the ballast water released by ships, including the Zebra Mussel, *Dreissena polymorpha*, which some ecologists consider to be the worst invader in the world.

Regardless of category, a species does not become invasive quickly. Ecologists have divided the time frame over which a species becomes invasive into a series of generalized stages. The first stage can be considered the colonizing event; whether intentional or not, this is when an exotic species is introduced into an area outside of its natural range. This introduction is followed by an establishment stage, where the introduced organism(s) find a suitable habitat and a consistent food source, survive, and successfully reproduce in this new habitat. Once it becomes established, an invasive species can increase its number and disperse to and colonize areas beyond the initial point of colonization. Usually, this is due to a lack of environmental or ecological constraints on the species. Also, during this stage, the species becomes noticed, and its invasiveness is realized. The final stage is more of a gray area. During this stage, invasive species start having significant ecological or economic impacts. For example, they may begin displacing native species and causing crop yields to drop. The time it takes an invasive species to reach the final stage is highly variable and depends on the many factors described earlier. Each instance of an invasive species worldwide is due to a unique combination of factors that aligned and allowed a particular species to become invasive in that specific environment and location.

Similarly, a unique combination of strategies is used against invasive species to halt their spread. Invasive species management uses these strategies to prevent, control, or eradicate species that have been introduced into an area outside of their natural range. Over time, and through much trial and error, a wide variety of methods have been developed to combat invasive species. Invariably, effective invasive species management requires a sustained, multipronged approach.

Prevention is the most effective and sustainable approach to invasive species management. Preventative measures include regulatory actions designed to prohibit the movement of organisms beyond their natural range and physical actions intended to detect and intercept organisms before they enter non-native areas. Regulatory and physical measures are often used with public information campaigns designed to increase awareness of particular invasive species and prevent further spread.

Once a species does become established and invasive, a more direct approach is needed to control or eradicate it, usually through the use of physical, chemical, and biological methods.

PHYSICAL control is the use of people or equipment to directly or indirectly affect the target species. Examples include hand-picking, mowing, girdling, hunting, and prescribed burning. The advantages of physical controls are that they usually directly target a specific individual, with minimal effects on non-targeted organisms. Furthermore, physical controls deliver immediate results and can quickly eradicate the targeted species from an area. Disadvantages are the associated labor and equipment costs, which can get rather expensive. Also, physical methods are usually only effective over a relatively small area.

CHEMICAL control is the use of specific chemicals to reduce the ability of the target organism to survive and thrive. Examples include herbicides and poisons. The advantages of chemical methods are that they are relatively inexpensive and usually fast acting. Disadvantages include potential toxicity to other species, cumulative effects, and the possibility of creating resistant strains of the target species.

BIOLOGICAL control is the use of other organisms, such as natural predators, parasites, or pathogens, to reduce the population of the target species. The advantages are that it is the safest of the three methods and often the most cost-effective. Disadvantages are that it usually takes a long time for the control species to become established and impact the target species and the unknown effects it may have on non-target species, and the ecosystem. These methods are not mutually exclusive; almost all invasive species management programs utilize many strategies and best practices.

This book will introduce you to 100 species considered invasive in North America. We include a brief description of the species, its native origin, where it is currently found in North America, when and how it arrived (if known), and the impacts it may cause ecologically and economically, as well as the strategies used to control or eradicate it (if any). Species are organized alphabetically by scientific name within a group, including animals (invertebrates, fish, amphibians, reptiles, birds, and mammals), plants, microorganisms (bacteria, fungi, and viruses), and others.

ANIMALS

INVERTEBRATES

Achatina fulica

GIANT AFRICAN LAND SNAIL

DESCRIPTION: A giant, distinctive snail with a long, conical shell. It can get up to 8 in. (20 cm) in length but is primarily found in the 2 to 4 in. (5 to 10 cm) range. The shell is usually light brown, with a variable amount of brown and white banding.

NATIVE DISTRIBUTION: It is native to eastern Africa.

NORTH AMERICAN DISTRIBUTION: It is present in many tropical and subtropical parts of North America, primarily in the Caribbean, and in Hawaii. It was formerly found in Florida, but it is believed to have been eradicated there.

DATE(S) AND MEANS OF INTRODUCTION: The Giant African Land Snail was first found in Florida in the 1960s and the Caribbean in the 1980s. It has been imported for use as a food resource, as a companion animal, or for medicinal purposes.

THREATS: It is a fast-growing snail, with a high reproductive capacity, that feeds on a variety of vegetation, including ornamental and agricultural species. It is also able to be easily transported, at any life stage, and can enter a dormant-like state in cold weather. Once it escapes, it reproduces vigorously. Many experts believe it is the most damaging land snail in the world. Besides the damage to crops and ornamental species, it also impacts native vegetation and their habitats, and outcompetes native snail species. It also is believed to be a vector of several plant diseases.

MANAGEMENT: Many methods have been tested and studied for eradicating this snail, much more so than most invasive species. The species experiences periodic population declines, and it can be challenging to assess if the occasional decrease in population is due to a specific control method or an external environmental factor. Historically, chemical treatments with molluscicides were the most common method; however, more recent research suggests these treatments do not effectively reduce snail populations. Various biological control methods have been tested, with limited success. Manual removal of snails has proven to be just as effective as existing chemical or biological control methods. Barriers, screens, and traps are also used as a way of limiting the movement of snails.

Adelges tsugae

HEMLOCK WOOLLY ADELGID

DESCRIPTION: Small, aphid-like insects that feed on hemlock (*Tsuga*) trees. Eggs are deposited in a white, woolly mass around 0.3 mm long. During autumn, immatures (nymphs) surround themselves with a cottony mass. Adults have a purplish-red coloration, reaching lengths of up to 0.75 mm. As they age, they cover themselves with a white, waxy coating.

NATIVE DISTRIBUTION: Hemlock Woolly Adelgids are native to China and Japan, and possibly western North America.

NORTH AMERICAN DISTRIBUTION: It has become established over a large portion of eastern North America, from Nova Scotia to northern Alabama, copying the range of native *Tsuga* trees. It can also be found in the Pacific Northwest.

DATE(S) AND MEANS OF INTRODUCTION: It was first recorded in 1951 in Virginia, found on ornamental hemlocks imported from Japan. The nursery trade is the primary spreader of the insect, with localized spreading caused by wind, birds, and humans.

THREATS: Both nymphs and adults feed on hemlock trees by sucking out sap from the stems. Insect feeding eventually leads to needle drop and overall loss of vigor and can cause the tree's death in as little as three years. It can feed on both cultivated and naturally growing hemlock species. It is estimated that about 25 percent of the area occupied by hemlocks in the United States has been infested. Hemlocks are essential components of the ecosystem, providing food and habitats to many species. The disappearance of hemlocks from their native range will have a far-reaching, cascading effect on ecosystems, ultimately decreasing biodiversity.

MANAGEMENT: Many physical, chemical, and biological control methods have been implemented to combat this species. These include implementing forestry techniques that benefit the health of hemlock trees, using pesticides, and releasing predatory insects that feed on the Hemlock Woolly Adelgid. Some states have quarantine measures in place to restrict the movement of hemlocks. The Forest Service has published a handbook for resource managers to refer to when making forest management decisions.

Aedes albopictus

ASIAN TIGER MOSQUITO

DESCRIPTION: A 5-mm-long mosquito, black with many white markings on its body and legs and a white stripe down the middle of its back.

NATIVE DISTRIBUTION: Its native range is from China to southeast Asia to Madagascar.

NORTH AMERICAN DISTRIBUTION: It can be found throughout most of North America, in areas with relatively mild winters. In the United States, it is primarily located south of a line from Delaware to Missouri.

DATE(S) AND MEANS OF INTRODUCTION: The earliest record of it in North America is from Trinidad and Tobago in 1983. The first U.S. record is from 1985. It is believed to have been spread via the international trade of tires, as Tiger Mosquitoes are known to lay eggs in rainwater accumulated inside tires stored outside.

THREATS: They are voracious biters and will bite many animals, including birds, lizards, amphibians, and mammals. They are also able to outcompete many other species of mosquito. The main threat, however, is that they are known vectors of several viruses that cause severe human diseases, including yellow fever, Rift Valley fever, dengue fever, and chikungunya.

MANAGEMENT: Many countries have established protocols for inspecting and treating various types of shipped goods to detect mosquitoes before they are transported into and around the country. Traditional mosquito traps are relatively ineffective in capturing this species, but new types of traps are being developed that show promise. Strains of male mosquitoes are being bioengineered that will result in nonviable offspring when mated with a wild female. A species of fungus is being studied as a potential biocontrol agent. And there are bacteria and chemicals readily available that can kill mosquito larvae where there is standing water.

Agrilus planipennis

EMERALD ASH BORER

DESCRIPTION: A metallic greenish-blue beetle, with a narrow body up to $^3/_5$ in. (15 mm) long. Larvae are white and grub-like, up to $1^2/_5$ in. (35 mm) long.

NATIVE DISTRIBUTION: It is native to eastern Russia, northern China, and the Korean Peninsula.

NORTH AMERICAN DISTRIBUTION: It is currently reported in at least 35 U.S. states (mainly in the Midwest and East) and five Canadian provinces. It is spreading rapidly.

DATE(S) AND MEANS OF INTRODUCTION: It was introduced into North America in 2002, in Detroit, Michigan, most likely in wood products imported from its native range. Further spread has been facilitated through the transport of wood for firewood or building materials.

THREATS: The larvae feed on tissues within stems and trunks, usually enough to kill the tree within 1 to 3 years. It is estimated that the Emerald Ash Borer has killed over 100 million trees in North America. It feeds primarily on ash (*Fraxinus*) species, and there is concern about the long-term survivability of several ash species. The ecological impact of this deforestation is monumental. Forests impacted by the Emerald Ash Borer are also more likely to be invaded by non-native plant species. The annual economic impact in the United States is estimated to be around $300 billion.

MANAGEMENT: Several strategies are used to prevent the spread and decrease the population density of the Emerald Ash Borer. Infected ash trees are usually easy to identify, due to the characteristic boring holes created by the larvae. Infected trees are cut down and then mechanically destroyed through chipping or burning. Insecticides may be applied to infected logs to prevent additional transmission. Insecticides can also be injected into the trunks of trees as either a preventative or curative measure. Biological control through parasitic insects and fungal species has been attempted in some areas, but its effectiveness has not been determined. Regulatory regimes include using quarantines for cut ash trees, prohibiting the removal of ash wood from infested areas, and regulating the sale of ash trees in the nursery trade.

Amynthas agrestis

ASIAN JUMPING WORM, CRAZY WORM

DESCRIPTION: A type of earthworm that lives amongst the leaf litter in forested areas. It is reddish to brown and can get up to 6¼ in. (160 mm) long and ⅓ in. (8 mm) wide. It tends to thrash around, or appear to jump, when it is disturbed, hence the common names. Due to variability within the species, and similarities to other species, it is difficult to identify correctly based on readily apparent features alone.

NATIVE DISTRIBUTION: It is native to Japan and the Korean Peninsula.

NORTH AMERICAN DISTRIBUTION: It is present in at least 25 U.S. states, from Texas to Minnesota and eastward, and one Canadian province.

DATE(S) AND MEANS OF INTRODUCTION: The details surrounding its introduction into North America are unknown. It was first identified in 1939, but there are records dating back to the late 1800s of Asian worms being found, although the species is unknown. They likely arrived as hitchhikers on plants being imported from Asia. Further spread has been facilitated by using this worm as fishing bait.

THREATS: The worms feed on soil and leaf litter, removing a significant amount of leaf litter from the forest floor. In areas with heavy infestations, the soil surface may be completely bare. Ultimately, this affects the structure and chemical composition of the soil, negatively impacting a wide variety of native species.

MANAGEMENT: Preventing further spread is the only viable option to manage Asian Jumping Worms. Management involves the public's participation in implementing practices that help reduce the spread, such as the proper disposal of bait worms, being careful not to accidentally transport soil, and reporting sightings of the worms to appropriate authorities.

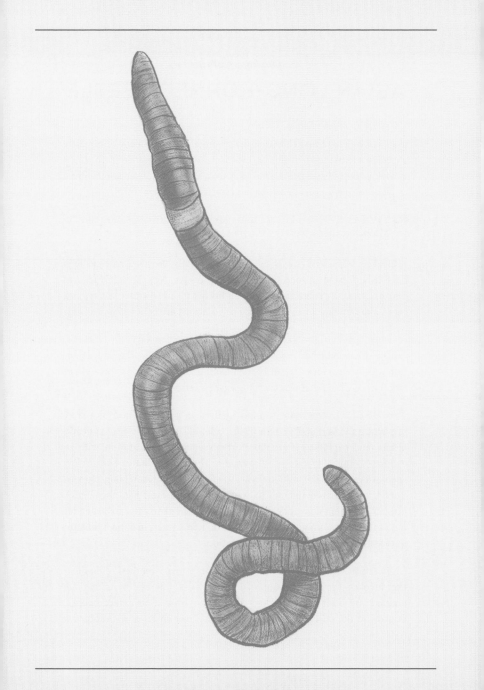

Anoplophora glabripennis

ASIAN LONG-HORNED BEETLE

DESCRIPTION: Adults are giant beetles, up to 1½ in. (4 cm) long, with long, curving antennae that are usually longer than the beetle's body. The antennae are made up of alternating black and white segments. The body is darkly colored and shiny, with various white or yellowish spots. Some or all of the leg segments can have a bluish-gray color.

NATIVE DISTRIBUTION: These beetles are native to China and the Korean Peninsula.

NORTH AMERICAN DISTRIBUTION: In North America, it is currently present in four states: Massachusetts, New York, Ohio, and South Carolina. There have been sightings in a few other states, and two Canadian provinces, but those populations are believed to be eradicated now.

DATE(S) AND MEANS OF INTRODUCTION: The first detection was in New York City, in 1996. It likely arrived via the importation of wood from China that was carrying eggs or larvae.

THREATS: Larvae bore tunnels (galleries) into the wood of a tree, impacting the vascular system of the tree, ultimately causing its death. Urban landscaping trees are the most susceptible to infestation, with an estimated mortality rate of 30 percent. The United States has already spent more than $250 million trying to eradicate the Asian Long-Horned Beetle. It is relatively difficult to detect an infestation, due to the beetle's lifestyle, as it remains hidden much of the time. Furthermore, the beetles tend to lay only a small number of eggs on many trees, making it difficult to discern the true extent of an infestation.

MANAGEMENT: In North America, the primary method of eradication involves the identification of infested trees, followed by immediate incineration and removal. Dogs have been trained to detect beetles, improving the odds of finding all infected trees in an area. Additional work is being done on creating hybrid trees resistant to the beetle. The United States and European countries have enacted regulations that require wood imported from China to be treated with pesticides to reduce the populations of Asian Long-Horned Beetles entering North America.

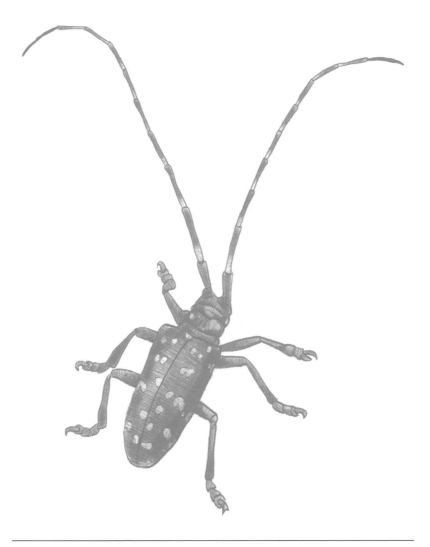

Apis mellifera spp. *scutellata*

AFRICANIZED HONEYBEE, KILLER BEE

DESCRIPTION: The Africanized Honeybee is a hybridization between European and African species of honeybees. As such, they are nearly indistinguishable from their nonhybridized counterparts without closely examining the size and color of specific body parts. Despite their similar appearance, Africanized Honeybees are noticeably more aggressive when defending their nest, with swarms sometimes reaching hundreds of bees. Comparatively, European Honeybee swarms typically only reach the size of 10 to 20 bees. The Africanized Honeybee's increased hostility and swarm size mean hives can quickly incapacitate or kill medium- to large-size mammals, including humans.

NATIVE DISTRIBUTION: There are several dozen subspecies of *Apis mellifera*, all native to different areas of Africa, Asia, or Europe; however, the Africanized Honeybee was hybridized and introduced by humans and therefore has no true native range.

NORTH AMERICAN DISTRIBUTION: First identified in the United States in Texas, it is now prevalent in California, Nevada, Utah, Arizona, New Mexico, Oklahoma, Louisiana, and Florida. It is predicted that populations could reach as far north as Illinois.

DATE(S) AND MEANS OF INTRODUCTION: Killer Bees were introduced into Brazil in the 1950s as part of a breeding project that aimed to combine the manageability of the European Honeybee with the hardiness of the African Honeybee. Unfortunately, the Africanized Honeybees escaped captivity into the wild before the project could be completed.

THREATS: Killer Bees threaten public safety and beekeepers' economic security in areas where they have been introduced. This species has been responsible for at least 1,000 human deaths since it was introduced into North America, and those numbers are increasing. The economic toll is also significant, as beekeepers note a substantial reduction in productivity in areas that the Africanized Honeybee has invaded.

MANAGEMENT: The strategies employed to prevent and control Killer Bee infestation depend on the environment and situation. This species is adapted to tropical climates, and migration into temperate climates is less common. In areas with a higher likelihood of Killer Bee infestation, prevention strategies should include awareness campaigns to educate the public about the characteristics of prime nesting structures. These can be removed or modified before nesting occurs. Beekeepers should requeen their hives annually to ensure they are not rearing Africanized Honeybees. New research on the behavior of Africanized Honeybees is underway to develop improved early warning systems.

Belonolaimus longicaudatus

STING NEMATODE

DESCRIPTION: A soil-dwelling plant-parasitic nematode that is no larger than 2 to 3 mm in length. It has a long stylet on its anterior end, which functions like a hypodermic needle and injects digestive fluids into a plant's roots.

NATIVE DISTRIBUTION: It is native to the southeastern portion of the United States, from Texas to Virginia, and is common in sandy soils along the Gulf of Mexico and Atlantic coasts.

NORTH AMERICAN DISTRIBUTION: The Sting Nematode has spread beyond its native range and has been detected as far north as Ohio and as far west as California. It has also been found on several Caribbean islands.

DATE(S) AND MEANS OF INTRODUCTION: It is unknown how and when the Sting Nematode was first introduced into uninfested locations in North America.

THREATS: It is a parasite of many types of crop plants, such as cotton, beets, and soybeans, as well as turfgrass and ornamental plants. It feeds on the roots and causes plants to have stunted growth, wilting, and a higher susceptibility to other pathogens. Severe infestations result in the plant's death. It is considered one of the most destructive plant-parasitic nematodes, causing an estimated $10 billion or more in annual crop loss.

MANAGEMENT: Regular monitoring of Sting Nematode populations present in the soil informs management decisions. Unless growers are actively testing for the Sting Nematode, detection usually occurs when the symptoms present themselves. By the time symptoms are observed, many seasons of avoidable crop loss may have already occurred. Sting Nematode populations are reduced by growing nonhost cover crops in fallow seasons or crop rotations, and this strategy should be employed in most Sting Nematode management plans. The application of nematicide is the most deployed control method, but biological control using bacteria has shown promise in managing the nematode.

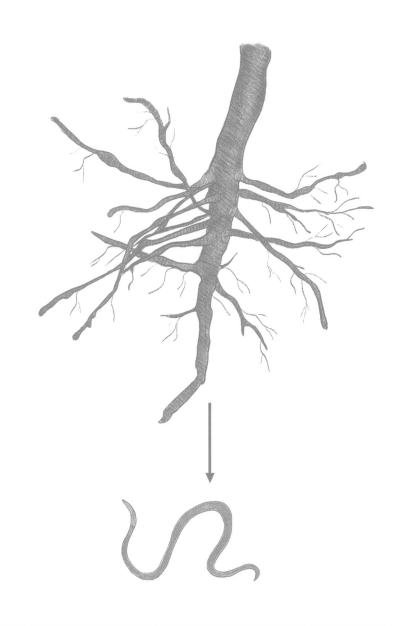

Bythotrephes longimanus

SPINY WATER FLEA

DESCRIPTION: A large species of crustacean zooplankton, which is distinguished by having a long tail spine, about twice as long as the body, having a total length of up to ³/₅ in. (15 mm).

NATIVE DISTRIBUTION: It has a wide distribution, from Europe to China.

NORTH AMERICAN DISTRIBUTION: It is found in the Great Lakes and in Lake Winnipeg in Manitoba. It is also becoming widespread in inland lakes in the states and provinces surrounding the Great Lakes.

DATE(S) AND MEANS OF INTRODUCTION: It was first detected in Lake Ontario in 1982 and was present in all Great Lakes within a few years. It is believed to have been transported from Europe, as dormant eggs in the ballast water of cargo ships.

THREATS: This is a predatory, carnivorous zooplankton that primarily feeds on smaller zooplankton, which happens to describe the native zooplankton in the Great Lakes. Thus, this predation results in a reduced population of native zooplankton, which affects higher trophic levels that depend on zooplankton. Because of its size and spine, some fish will avoid trying to eat this species. Those that do are at risk of injury and possibly death from the spine. This leads to a decrease in the population of planktivorous fish in a body of water, which tend to be a favored food source for larger game fish. Lastly, the spines on these zooplankton are known to ruin fishing lines.

MANAGEMENT: There is currently no effective means of controlling or eradicating this species. Hot water treatments can kill Spiny Water Fleas attached to fishing gear and boating equipment, but unless this tactic is used at every boat landing on water bodies where it is found, it will have little to no effect on the spread of the species.

Cimex lectularius

BED BUG, COMMON BED BUG

DESCRIPTION: The Bed Bug has five larval stages and an adult stage. The appearance is somewhat similar for all stages. The most significant distinction is color, which transitions from tan in the larval stages to reddish brown in the adult stage and increases in size with each instar (the phase between successive molts). Adult Bed Bugs are about $^1/_5$ in. (0.5 cm) long, with a flat, oval body covered with tiny hairs. Like all "true bugs" (organisms in the order Hemiptera), they have sucking mouthparts, sometimes called a beak.

NATIVE DISTRIBUTION: It is native to Europe.

NORTH AMERICAN DISTRIBUTION: The Bed Bug is found throughout the entire North American continent.

DATE(S) AND MEANS OF INTRODUCTION: European settlers likely brought the Bed Bug to North America in the 17th century. The Bed Bug was found across the North American continent by the late 1800s but was nearly eradicated in North America by the 1930s through fastidious hygiene and prevention. With the onset of WWII and the rise in international travel, the Bed Bug reinfested most of North America by the 1950s.

THREATS: The Bed Bug is a bloodsucking insect that feeds on sleeping humans. Bed Bugs typically feed for 5 to 10 minutes a few times each week, and a heavily infested bed can harbor thousands of bloodsucking Bed Bugs! They are known to host human pathogens, but the transmission of diseases to humans is very unlikely. The only confirmed pathogen vectored and transmitted by Bed Bugs is *Pasteurella multocida*, which may cause cellulitis. Excessive and continued blood loss from bites can lead to chronic anemia in extreme cases.

MANAGEMENT: New infestations are often caused by travel. Insects can be harbored in in clothing and bedding, and even in hair. Good personal hygiene and washing all clothing and bedding in very hot water before using them is the most effective way to prevent spread. Infestations can be identified by dark fecal stains in the corners and edges of mattresses. Bed Bugs also have a characteristic sickly sweet odor that can be detected in heavy infestations.

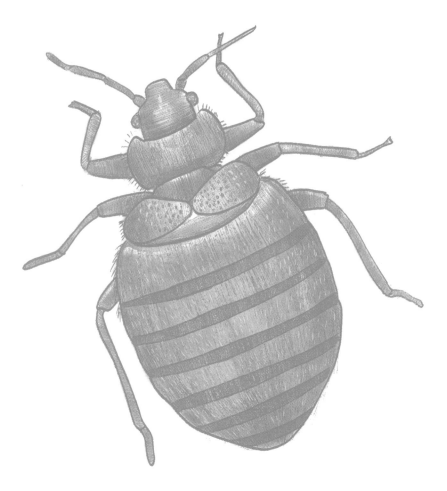

Coptotermes formosanus

FORMOSAN TERMITE

DESCRIPTION: A colonial, social insect that feeds on cellulose-containing materials, such as wood. A mature colony can have several million individuals and produce 1,000 eggs per day. The colony is made up of workers, soldiers, and reproductive castes. While there are notable differences between the castes, Formosan Termites are all small (~²/₅ in. [1 cm] long), soft-bodied insects with a yellowish-white color. They tend to live underground but are known to invade houses, utility poles, and other wood structures.

NATIVE DISTRIBUTION: It is native to southern China. While not specific to any habitat, it is chiefly found in moist locations and near wooded areas.

NORTH AMERICAN DISTRIBUTION: In North America, it is found in the Caribbean islands, and the following U.S. states: Alabama, California, Florida, Georgia, Hawaii, Louisiana, Mississippi, North and South Carolina, Tennessee, and Texas. It is limited by cold temperatures, and it is unlikely to advance as far north as the 35th parallel (southern Virginia).

DATE(S) AND MEANS OF INTRODUCTION: Newspaper reports indicate that it was first discovered in Hawaii in 1869, and the first continental U.S. appearance appears to be in Houston in 1965. It is thought that the Formosan Termite was introduced through imported wood and plant materials from infested areas.

THREATS: It is one of the most destructive insect pests in the United States. It can feed on various woody plants, wood structures, and non-cellulose-containing materials like plastic. In as little as two years, Formosan Termites can cause severe structural damage to a house, usually going unnoticed until it is too late. It is estimated that over $1 billion is spent annually in the United States on prevention, eradication, and repairs related to this species. Ecological impacts include the loss of biodiversity through the killing of native trees and the fact they can outcompete native species of termites, which are far less destructive.

MANAGEMENT: A variety of strategies can be used against this termite. Using treated lumber for building materials prevents termite infestations. Chemical barriers can be applied around structures that are susceptible to termite infestation. Termiticides can be sprayed on construction sites before starting construction. Wood mulch and firewood should never be placed up against a suscep-tible structure. Structures with moisture issues (leaky plumb-ing, etc.) should be repaired.

Dreissena polymorpha

ZEBRA MUSSEL

DESCRIPTION: Zebra Mussels are small, triangular mollusks about the size of a fingernail. They have characteristic brown-and-white stripes patterning on their shell surface.

NATIVE DISTRIBUTION: Zebra Mussels are native to the seas of Eastern Europe.

NORTH AMERICAN DISTRIBUTION: They are found throughout the Great Lakes and in freshwater bodies of Texas, Oklahoma, Colorado, California, Utah, and Nevada.

DATE(S) AND MEANS OF INTRODUCTION: The mussels were first brought to North America in the 1980s via ballast water in ships traveling from Russia to the United States.

THREATS: The Zebra Mussel was described as "the worst aquatic invader in the world" by the Centre for Agriculture and Bioscience International (CABI). Zebra Mussels deploy protein strands called byssal threads to attach themselves to solid surfaces, living or nonliving. They bind to other mussels, preventing them from moving and feeding, and to solid structures like water intake pipes, causing significant damage to infrastructure. The Zebra Mussel is a filter feeder and rapidly clears water of algae and other consumables. The cleared water and altered food chain reduce native species' biodiversity in habitats where the Zebra Mussel becomes established.

MANAGEMENT: Preventing new locations from becoming infested is accomplished through education campaigns focused on informing lake users on how to identify and remove Zebra Mussels from boats and docks before introducing them to new bodies of water. Monitoring and surveillance programs are in place to quickly eradicate potential new infestations before populations become too large to manage.

Faxonius rusticus

RUSTY CRAYFISH

DESCRIPTION: Large crayfish up to 4 in. (10 cm) long. The body is usually a brownish-green color, with rust-brown spots along the side. Under certain conditions, the spots may not be discernible. Their pincers have a black band around the tips.

NATIVE DISTRIBUTION: It is native to the Ohio River Basin in the United States.

NORTH AMERICAN DISTRIBUTION: It has spread to at least 19 U.S. states, primarily in the midwestern and eastern parts of the country, as well as at least three Canadian provinces.

DATE(S) AND MEANS OF INTRODUCTION: The first reports of it outside the Ohio River Basin are from 1957 in Wisconsin. The first Canadian report is from 1963, in Manitoba. It has spread primarily due to humans, who have introduced it as a bait source for anglers, to control aquatic vegetation, or for food harvesting.

THREATS: It is an aggressive species with a voracious appetite, feeding on aquatic vegetation, fish eggs, and invertebrates. It outcompetes native crayfish and is known to hybridize with some of them. This results in a loss of biodiversity and population size of native species, including popular sport fish. The annual impact on fish populations is estimated to be $1.5 million for one county in Wisconsin.

MANAGEMENT: Prevention strategies use public awareness campaigns and regulations in many U.S. states and Canadian provinces prohibiting the possession or commerce of this species. Control methods include structures meant to limit their spread, such as dams and weirs, the deployment of baited traps, managing fish species that prey on crayfish, and using chemical control methods. As with most invasive species, a combination of strategies provides the most effective results.

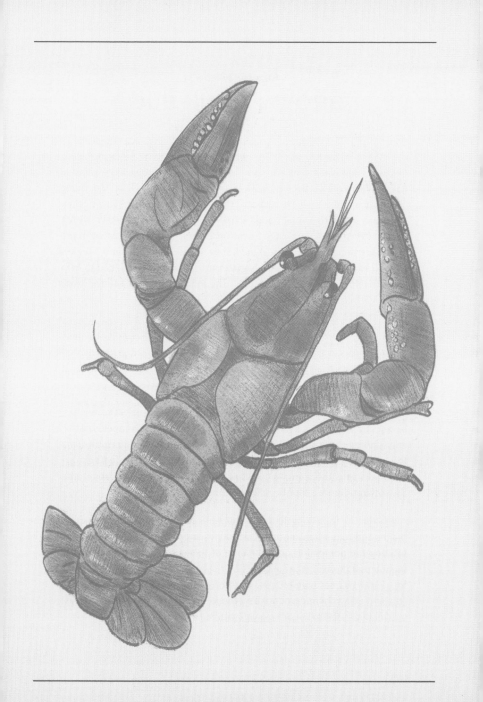

Halyomorpha halys

BROWN STINK BUG, STINK BUG, MARMORATED STINK BUG

DESCRIPTION: Brown Stink Bugs are "true bugs" in the order Hemiptera. They have five nymphal (immature) stages. At maturity, they are dime size with a shield body shape. They are typically brown with a few scattered white markings. Scent-producing glands are located in the Stink Bug thorax. When threatened, they release chemicals into a region of their exoskeleton called the evapatorium, a structure designed to help quickly release the scent molecules. The foul, acrid smell emitted from the Stink Bug's body repels predators.

NATIVE DISTRIBUTION: They are native to China, Japan, South Korea, and Taiwan.

NORTH AMERICAN DISTRIBUTION: The Stink Bug has been reported in nearly every U.S. state, Mexico, and parts of Canada. It is considered a severe agricultural and nuisance pest along the entire Eastern Seaboard.

DATE(S) AND MEANS OF INTRODUCTION: Stink Bugs were first reported in Allentown, Pennsylvania, in 1998. It is speculated that they stowed away in shipping containers, but the validity of this claim is uncertain.

THREATS: The Stink Bug has a wide host range but causes particularly significant damage to high-value fruit and nut trees. The estimated potential crop loss is staggering, with some fruit growers losing 90 percent of their harvest during periods of heavy Stink Bug infestations. Stink Bugs also attack a variety of vegetable crops and grapes. One additional concern, primarily in the grape industry, is "Stink Bug taint"—the acrid taste and smell that is left behind following a Stink Bug invasion.

MANAGEMENT: Controlling Stink Bug infestations is very challenging. Because this is a relatively new pest with the capacity to damage many different crops, management strategies will vary. Several biocontrol organisms that parasitize Stink Bug egg sacs are under development and show promise. Chemical control options exist, but insecticides may be challenging or impossible to use in some industries and disrupt existing integrated pest management (IPM) plans.

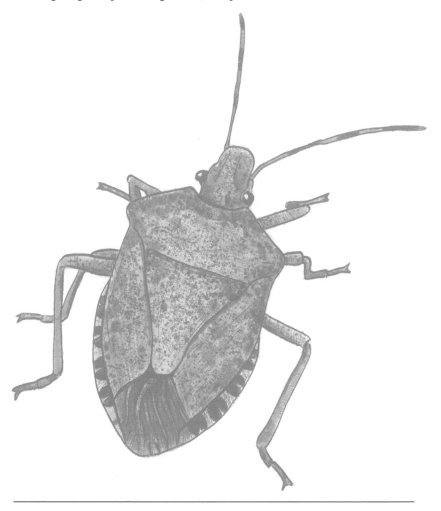

Lycorma delicatula

SPOTTED LANTERN FLY

DESCRIPTION: A species of planthopper that ranges in length from $^3/_5$ to 1¼ in. (15 to 30 mm). The front wings are gray, with many black spots and distinctive reticulate venation over the outer portion. The hind wings are black, white, and red, with additional black spots on the red part. Superficially, it resembles a moth. Nymphs start black, with white spots, but become primarily red during the final instar (the phase between successive molts). Superficially, they resemble spiders. They tend to be gregarious and are often seen in large numbers on a single tree.

NATIVE DISTRIBUTION: It is native to China and Southeast Asia.

NORTH AMERICAN DISTRIBUTION: It is currently found in nine U.S. states, from Indiana to New England and the mid-Atlantic.

DATE(S) AND MEANS OF INTRODUCTION: It was first discovered in Pennsylvania in 2014, although it is believed to have been present for several years before it was reported. The means of introduction is unknown, but it is theorized that it came via egg masses attached to items imported from Asia. The egg masses are cryptically colored and often challenging to see.

THREATS: Nymphs and adults are known to feed on over 100 different species of plants. Many of these species are important crops and ornamentals. If populations are high enough, host species can become weakened or killed outright, altering the species composition of that ecosystem. Furthermore, as they feed, they secrete honeydew, which can lead to sooty mold infections. Economic impacts could become significant if populations continue to increase and spread.

MANAGEMENT: Various management methods are used in the United States. These include social strategies, such as public awareness campaigns and quarantining susceptible products. Several pesticides are effective in killing eggs, nymphs, and adults. Other methods include manually destroying egg masses, sanitizing products that may have egg masses, and wrapping trees with adhesive tape to prevent egg laying.

Lymantria dispar

SPONGY MOTH

DESCRIPTION: A gray-colored moth with darker wing markings, with a wingspan of up to 2¾ in. (7 cm). Caterpillars are covered with bristly hairs and have red and blue markings on their backs.

NATIVE DISTRIBUTION: It is native to much of Europe, Asia, and North Africa.

NORTH AMERICAN DISTRIBUTION: The Spongy Moth has become established in the eastern United States and Canada.

DATE(S) AND MEANS OF INTRODUCTION: It was accidentally introduced into Massachusetts in 1869 and reached Canada by 1924.

THREATS: The caterpillar is a voracious consumer and can eat a broad range of deciduous tree species. It also tends to lay eggs on human-created items, resulting in further spread. During outbreaks, which can last multiple years, entire trees can become defoliated by the caterpillars. While most trees would be able to survive occasional infestations, repeated outbreaks will result in the death of those trees affected. Since 1924, Spongy Moths have defoliated more than 91.4 million acres (37 million hectares) of forest in the United States.

MANAGEMENT: An intensive, multipronged strategy is in place to combat the spread of this species. Every year, more than 300,000 traps are placed around the United States for monitoring and detection purposes. Other strategies include implementing forestry practices that reduce the spread and utilizing several methods of biological, chemical, and mechanical control.

Neodiprion sertifer

EUROPEAN PINE SAWFLY

DESCRIPTION: A pine needle–eating species of sawfly. Adults are approximately ²/₅ in. (1 cm) long and either reddish brown or black. Males have prominent feathery antennae, while females have slender, serrated antennae. The caterpillar-like larvae get up to 1 in. (25 mm) in length, are grayish green in color, and develop black stripes and spots as they age. Large numbers of larvae on pine trees from spring to midsummer indicate signs of an infestation. They feed primarily on older needles, often consuming all of a tree's older needles. The sawfly favors mainly the two-needled pines, especially Scotch pine (*Pinus sylvestris*) and mugo pine (*Pinus mugo*), but has been observed on many other species.

NATIVE DISTRIBUTION: It has a broad native range, from Europe to Korea and Japan.

NORTH AMERICAN DISTRIBUTION: It is found in the eastern provinces of Canada and in the United States in an area from Montana east to Maine.

DATE(S) AND MEANS OF INTRODUCTION: It was first seen in New Jersey in 1925, and quickly spread to its current range. It most likely arrived via imported nursery stock.

THREATS: Because they only feed on older needles, infestations are rarely fatal to a tree. However, repeated infestations over multiple years can weaken a tree enough to cause its death. The European Pine Sawfly is a serious pest to the Christmas tree industry, as even a small outbreak can defoliate a tree to the point that it is unlikely to be selected by anyone to be their Christmas tree.

MANAGEMENT: The primary way this species is controlled is by using a virus as a biological control agent. In fact, this virus (called NsNPV) is one of the most successful biological control agents that have been developed. Other biological control methods have been attempted with varying levels of success, including bacteria and nematodes. In small forests or stands, manual removal and destruction is a feasible option, because the larvae colonies are easily detected. Pheromone-baited traps have been used, with variable success, in several areas of the world. This species is also susceptible to many types of insecticides, which are typically applied through aerial spraying.

Platydemus manokwari

NEW GUINEA FLATWORM

DESCRIPTION: A large flatworm, up to 2¾ in. (7 cm) long, that is widest in the middle and tapers to both ends. It is olive brown, with white stripes, and has two large eyes on the back of the head.

NATIVE DISTRIBUTION: It is believed to be native to New Guinea.

NORTH AMERICAN DISTRIBUTION: Since it was discovered in 1962, it has spread to many Pacific islands, including Hawaii.

DATE(S) AND MEANS OF INTRODUCTION: It was used as a biocontrol agent of land snails, which certainly facilitated its spread, but it is also readily transported in plants and soils, and much of its spread is accidental. It was first discovered in Hawaii in 1992.

THREATS: They are predatory flatworms that can significantly impact the native snails where they occur, potentially leading to extinction. It is thought that they may feed on other soil organisms, such as earthworms. They are also a host for a nematode that can cause severe human disease.

MANAGEMENT: Preventing new infestations is the most critical aspect of management. A quarantine system is in place for incoming and outgoing plant material to prevent the transport of flatworms to new locations. Plant material is also visually inspected for signs of flatworms. Soil is subjected to hot water treatment, effectively killing adult flatworms.

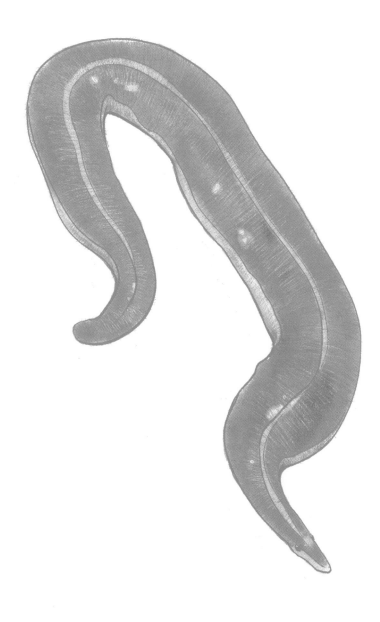

Solenopsis invicta

RED IMPORTED FIRE ANT, RIFA

DESCRIPTION: A reddish-brown ant named for the painful burning caused by its sting.

NATIVE DISTRIBUTION: It is native to central South America.

NORTH AMERICAN DISTRIBUTION: It is found in Mexico and the southeastern United States.

DATE(S) AND MEANS OF INTRODUCTION: It was first reported in 1929 in Mobile, Alabama. Population densities increased in the 1940s and 1950s. It was possibly introduced as an accidental stowaway in baggage traveling from Argentina to the United States.

THREATS: The RIFA sting is venomous and moderately to excruciatingly painful. They cause a significant problem for livestock animals and wildlife, as Red Imported Fire Ants typically work as a unit, surrounding and stinging other insects, lizards, and small mammals that may be threats or food sources. The United States spends approximately $1 billion annually in activities to prevent and control RIFAs.

MANAGEMENT: Effective management options are somewhat limited. Research into organisms that can be employed as biocontrol agents is underway, but none are yet available for widespread application. Some modifications to cultural practices may reduce ant populations or minimize their impact. For example, planning calving to occur during timelines that avoid summer months, when ants are most active, prevents livestock loss. The most effective management strategy is the direct injection of colonies with insecticides. Any chemical management plan should emphasize killing the queen to prevent new eggs from being produced.

Varroa destructor

VARROA MITE

DESCRIPTION: Varroa Mites are spiderlike organisms that are invisible to the naked eye. Their bodies are oval shaped, with a shiny, smooth, white-colored appearance. The legs and body are hirsute (hairy), and their mouthparts are beak-like.

NATIVE DISTRIBUTION: The Varroa Mite is native to Korea, Japan, and Thailand.

NORTH AMERICAN DISTRIBUTION: It is found in Canada, Costa Rica, Cuba, Mexico, and the United States.

DATE(S) AND MEANS OF INTRODUCTION: It was first found in the United States in 1987 and is now widespread throughout the North American continent.

THREATS: Varroa Mites are bloodsucking parasites of honeybees, causing a disease called varroosis. The mites feed on adults and larvae using their piercing, beak-like mouthparts. The continual loss of blood eventually leads to weakened bee populations, and wounds create entry points for bacterial, fungal, and viral pathogens. Severe infestations can wipe out the entire hive. The mites can spread quickly from bee to bee and hive to hive. Impacts are monetary and ecological, due to the overall decrease in commercial honey production and the reduction in active pollination.

MANAGEMENT: There is currently no method to completely eradicate the mites from infested hives. A complex, multipronged approach is used to reduce mite populations. Commercial honey producers' management strategies to reduce the mite population include limiting mite access to combs by using open screen floors, using fresh combs each season, and using an "artificial swarm" strategy to move parent colonies and disrupt mite infestation. Some biocontrol strategies include the introduction of natural enemies—for instance, a pseudoscorpion that eats mites. Chemical control agents exist, but mites often become resistant to chemical control methods, and the chemicals that control mites are sometimes toxic to bees and other insects. Fungal and bacterial control agents are in development that may provide safer options in the future.

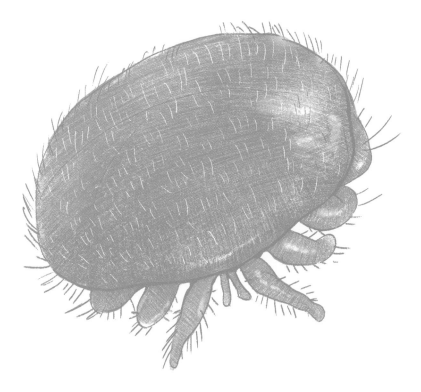

Wasmannia auropunctata

LITTLE FIRE ANT, ELECTRIC ANT

DESCRIPTION: The worker ants, which are most often encountered, are usually a light golden-brown color, and are 1 to 2 mm long. The body is sparsely covered by long hairs. This species does not build a mound, but nests in a wide variety of places, natural and man-made.

NATIVE DISTRIBUTION: It is native to Central and South America.

NORTH AMERICAN DISTRIBUTION: Non-native distribution in North America is primarily in California, Florida, and Hawaii in the United States, and British Columbia, Manitoba, Ontario, and Quebec in Canada.

DATE(S) AND MEANS OF INTRODUCTION: It was first discovered in Florida in 1924, where it was likely introduced inadvertently as a hitchhiker in soil, on plants, or in logs.

THREATS: They are aggressive ants that feed on invertebrates and small vertebrates and have been shown to deplete populations of spiders and overall reduce the invertebrate diversity in areas they infest. They promote and protect agricultural pests like aphids, which produce honeydew that the ants consume. They have an excruciating sting that can leave long-lasting welts on humans and cause blindness in smaller animals, including cats and dogs.

MANAGEMENT: Ant baits and poisons are often used, and can be quite effective; however, they are indiscriminate and will kill other ants that are also present. Early detection and quarantine are the most effective ways to prevent spreading; however, this requires constant surveillance and a rapid response to newly discovered colonies.

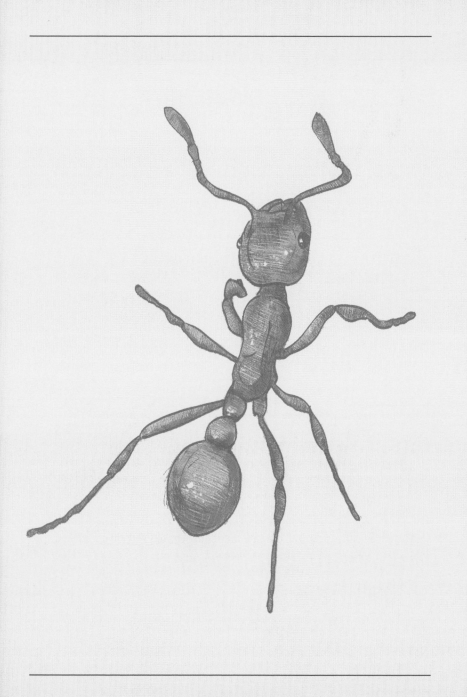

FISH

Channa argus

NORTHERN SNAKEHEAD, SNAKEHEAD FISH, RAIGYO

DESCRIPTION: A species of fish that is distinguished by its long, slender shape, with a very long dorsal fin that extends from the tail to near the head. The body is tan to brown in color, and is covered by dark, irregular splotches. Their mouths are large, extending well behind the eyes, and are filled with sharp teeth. They are known to get up to 59 in. (150 cm) long, but are rarely found over 40 in. (100 cm).

NATIVE DISTRIBUTION: This fish is native to Eastern Russia, the Korean Peninsula, and China.

NORTH AMERICAN DISTRIBUTION: It is found in eight U.S. states, from Maine to North Carolina, Florida, Arkansas, and California.

DATE(S) AND MEANS OF INTRODUCTION: It was first discovered in California in 1997. The scattered distribution in the United States suggests intentional releases of these fish into the water bodies they are found in, most likely from live food markets.

THREATS: It is an aggressive, voracious predator, feeding primarily on other fish. It can breathe air and survive out of water for up to four days, allowing it to move short distances over land to colonize a new body of water. Once established in a water body, it significantly alters the species composition because it will eat many fish, which has a cascading effect through the food web.

MANAGEMENT: Public awareness campaigns and governmental regulation are the primary prevention strategies. Fishermen are educated on the ecological impact caused by Northern Snakeheads and are trained to keep and freeze any they catch. Since October 2002, importing and transporting this species in the United States has been illegal. Established populations in smaller bodies of water can be killed off with nonselective piscicides. In larger bodies of water and rivers, control becomes more difficult. Mechanical control techniques such as electrofishing and trapping are used in some locations to reduce populations.

Gymnocephalus cernua

RUFFE, POPE

DESCRIPTION: A small to medium fish reaching about 10 in. (25 cm) in length. It is described as having the shape of a perch (*Perca*) and the markings of a walleye (*Sander*). They are olive brown with yellowish-white underbellies.

NATIVE DISTRIBUTION: The native range of Ruffe is broad, covering much of Europe and parts of Asia.

NORTH AMERICAN DISTRIBUTION: The Ruffe is found in Lake Superior, Lake Huron, and Lake Michigan.

DATE(S) AND MEANS OF INTRODUCTION: It was first identified in western Lake Superior in 1981. Genetic analysis determined this founding population likely originated from an invasive population located in the Elbe River in Germany and brought to the Great Lakes in ship ballast water.

THREATS: The Ruffe competes with several native fish species for space and resources. Minimum impact models predict at least a $24 million decrease in recreational fishing benefits annually as a consequence of decreased native fish populations.

MANAGEMENT: Due to the invasion of *G. cernua*, several new regulations have been established requiring all ships carrying ballast to flush their ballast tanks before entering the Great Lakes. These regulations were enacted by both the United States and Canada and should eliminate new invasions by *G. cernua*.

Hypophthalmichthys molitrix

SILVER CARP

DESCRIPTION: A freshwater fish in the minnow family, weighing up to 110 lbs. (50 kg). Mature individuals are typically large, robust fish, primarily silvery in color throughout their body, with no discernible markings, such as spots. The eyes are set relatively low on the head, about in the same plane as its mouth, which is toothless and slightly upturned. The lateral line has a distinctive downward curve over its abdominal region, and the tail fin is deeply forked. The species is noteworthy for its ability to leap out of the water (up to 3 m) when startled.

NATIVE DISTRIBUTION: It is found in freshwater river systems in China and adjacent parts of Russia, where it is primarily a plankton feeder.

NORTH AMERICAN DISTRIBUTION: Due to its popularity in aquaculture, it has been introduced worldwide. In North America, it is found in Mexico and the United States, primarily in the Mississippi River and its larger tributaries.

DATE(S) AND MEANS OF INTRODUCTION: It was first introduced into Arkansas in 1973 to control plankton populations in aquaculture ponds.

THREATS: Ecologically, Silver Carp can often outcompete native fish for habitats and food. It can significantly alter the plankton population and composition in a water body, affecting native planktivores, such as juvenile fish and mussels. Economically, the presence of Silver Carp will likely affect commercial fishing operations by depleting the populations of native fish. Efforts to prevent the spread of this species are also expensive: $10 million has been spent on electronic barriers to prevent them from getting into the Great Lakes.

MANAGEMENT: Prevention and control strategies include campaigns to educate the public about the impacts of Silver Carp and regulations prohibiting the import, transport, and acquisition of Silver Carp without a permit. In 2007, the U.S. Fish and Wildlife Service added it to the injurious wildlife list. Besides the electronic barrier mentioned earlier, another barrier control strategy is infusing carbon dioxide into the water at strategic locations.

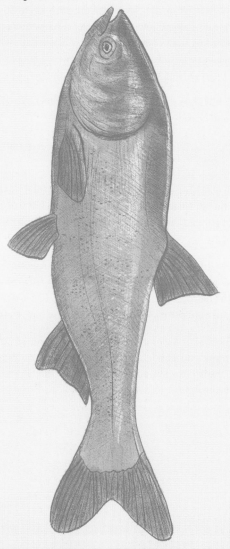

Neogobius melanostomus

ROUND GOBY

DESCRIPTION: A small bottom-dwelling fish, up to 10 in. (25 cm) in length. It typically has a yellowish-gray coloration, with blotches along its sides, but breeding males become primarily black, with white fin edges. The fish has a large head with prominent protruding eyeballs. A characteristic suction disk is on the lower surface of the pelvic fins.

NATIVE DISTRIBUTION: It is native to Eastern Europe and Asia, in freshwater and coastal habitats.

NORTH AMERICAN DISTRIBUTION: It is found in the Great Lakes and in some Great Lakes tributaries.

DATE(S) AND MEANS OF INTRODUCTION: It was first found in 1990, in the St. Clair River in Ontario. By 1993, it had been found in all the Great Lakes. It likely entered the Great Lakes via the ballast water of cargo ships.

THREATS: It feeds on the eggs of native fish species, especially lake trout (*Salvelinus namaycush*) and lake sturgeon (*Acipenser fulvescens*), impacting the reproductive rate of those species. It also outcompetes and displaces native bottom-dwelling fish species, such as sculpins.

MANAGEMENT: A combination of tactics and strategies is used, including traps and barriers, chemical treatments, regulations governing the transportation and commerce of this species, and public education campaigns.

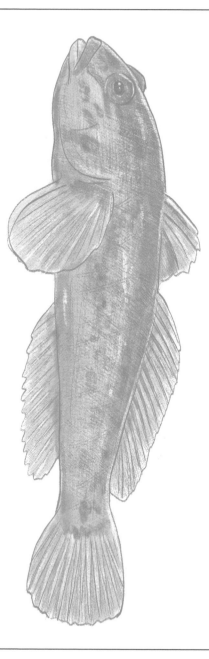

Petromyzon marinus

SEA LAMPREY

DESCRIPTION: A species of jawless fish that is snake- or eellike in appearance. They can get up to 40 in. (1 m) in length and weigh up to 5¹/₅ lbs. (2.5 kg). The mouth is rudimentary and has a spherical opening lined with numerous thornlike teeth. The body is colored bluish gray, with metallic purple coloring along its sides. There is usually a dark marbling or splotching across the body. Some other distinguishing characteristics are that they lack scales, have two dorsal fins, and have seven gill slits on each side of the head, like a shark.

NATIVE DISTRIBUTION: It is native to both Atlantic coasts, in North America and Europe.

NORTH AMERICAN DISTRIBUTION: In North America, it can be found as a non-native species in the Great Lakes and some of their tributaries. There is some disagreement over whether or not it is native to Lake Ontario.

DATE(S) AND MEANS OF INTRODUCTION: It was first discovered in Lake Ontario in 1835 and was in all the Great Lakes by 1946. It most likely entered the Great Lakes through the canal system connecting them to the Atlantic Ocean. Further spread may occur because it is used as bait by some anglers.

THREATS: They are voracious parasites on fish, using their disklike mouth and teeth to attach, like a leech, and eat away at the fish's body. They also produce a fluid in their mouth that acts as an anticoagulant on the fish's blood. Ultimately, a parasitized fish dies from blood loss. Populations of large, predatory fish in the Great Lakes have been significantly impacted by these lampreys, causing a domino effect on the Great Lakes' food web. The extirpation/extinction of three species of fish in the Great Lakes is at least partially attributable to Sea Lampreys.

MANAGEMENT: Controlling the Sea Lamprey requires a multifaceted program. A trapping and barrier system was implemented to prevent upstream migration and spawning. Sterilization of male Sea Lampreys is integrated into the trapping system. Male Sea Lampreys are trapped when trying to migrate upstream, sterilized, and released. Sterile males compete with unsterilized males for females and reduce overall fertilization and future offspring. Some chemical control has been attempted, and while it effectively removed 90 percent of the Sea Lamprey population in some areas, it is also harmful to other fish.

Pterois volitans and Pterois miles

LIONFISH

DESCRIPTION: It is a medium-size fish weighing about 2¼ lbs. (1 kg) and about 8 in. (20 cm) long. The fins and body are typically zebra striped and may have red, brown, or white stripes. Long, showy, venomous fin spikes line the dorsal side.

NATIVE DISTRIBUTION: Lionfish are native to the Indian and western Pacific Oceans.

NORTH AMERICAN DISTRIBUTION: It has breeding populations in the Caribbean and the East Coast of the United States.

DATE(S) AND MEANS OF INTRODUCTION: The exact source of Lionfish introduction to non-native regions is unknown. There is speculation that it was released into the coastal waters of Florida in 1992 when Hurricane Andrew destroyed several public aquariums. Still, there is limited evidence to support these claims, and there are reports of invasive Lionfish in Florida dating back to 1985.

THREATS: Lionfish have a significant impact on populations of native coral reef fish species. They are voracious eaters that consume all food sources and reproduce throughout the year. Females can produce up to 50,000 eggs every three days. They pose a moderate threat to human health via venomous spines, though fatal stings are very rare.

MANAGEMENT: Prevention and control strategies are regionally developed and not consistently deployed. In coastal areas of Florida, control strategies have primarily focused on employing or encouraging divers to hunt and remove Lionfish from localized areas. A Lionfish trapping system is under development but not yet widely deployed.

AMPHIBIANS

Rana catesbeiana

AMERICAN BULLFROG

DESCRIPTION: A large frog (up to 8 in. [20 cm] long) with mostly smooth skin. The coloration ranges from olive to green to brown, with the head noticeably paler. Dark splotches and spots may be seen on the back and legs. The tympanum (eardrum) is large and conspicuous. The male frog's low, loud, booming croak gives it the common name "bullfrog."

NATIVE DISTRIBUTION: It is native to the eastern part of North America, from Nova Scotia to Ontario, south to the east coast of Mexico.

NORTH AMERICAN DISTRIBUTION: It has been introduced into parts of North America where it is not considered native, in western North America and in the Caribbean.

DATE(S) AND MEANS OF INTRODUCTION: In the late 1800s and early 1900s, bullfrogs were introduced into many localities outside of their native range, primarily to raise them as a food source for humans.

THREATS: The biggest danger that bullfrogs pose is the negative effects they have on a variety of native species. Bullfrogs are voracious feeders on a variety of organisms, such as insects, birds, fish, and other frogs. They have a high reproductive capacity and are also more resilient than other types of frogs when it comes to environmental conditions, meaning they can withstand a wider range of fluctuations in temperature and water chemistry. They are also carriers of *Batrachochytrium dendrobatidis* (Bd) and the amphibian-infecting fungus described later in this book (see page 192).

MANAGEMENT: A variety of methods can be employed to combat bullfrog infestation. Biological controls consist of using a variety of species (fungi, leeches, aquatic insects, etc.) that prey on eggs, tadpoles, and juvenile frogs. Chemical controls may be used, but only in dire situations, because chemicals that will affect bullfrogs will also affect native species. If bullfrogs are to be "farmed" for human consumption, barriers can be put in place that at least contain the bullfrogs within the pond or lake in which they are being farmed.

Rhinella marina

CANE TOAD

DESCRIPTION: Stocky toads that reach a maximum length of 6 to 12 in. (15 to 30 cm). The skin may be tan, green, brown, or black, and conspicuously warty. Prominent, venomous parotid glands are located above the shoulder and behind the tympanum.

NATIVE DISTRIBUTION: They are native from southern Texas to northern South America.

NORTH AMERICAN DISTRIBUTION: In North America, they can be found in Hawaii, Florida, Puerto Rico, and many of the Caribbean Islands.

DATE(S) AND MEANS OF INTRODUCTION: Cane Toads were brought to many countries to be used as a biocontrol agent against several pests on sugarcane and other tropical crop plants. The earliest record in North America is from Jamaica in 1844. They were in Cuba by 1920 and Hawaii by 1932.

THREATS: They are highly versatile when it comes to habitat type, and they compete with native amphibians for food and habitats while consuming a wide variety of native fauna. They also have a toxic secretion that can be fatal to many animals, including humans.

MANAGEMENT: The primary prevention strategy for Cane Toads is through quarantine checks and regulations requiring permits for the ownership, exhibition, and transport of Cane Toads. Cane Toads cannot pass over a barrier at least 19¾ in. (50 cm) in height, and many "toad fences" have been constructed to limit their movement. Biological control agents are currently being studied.

REPTILES

Boiga irregularis

BROWN TREE SNAKE, BROWN CAT SNAKE

DESCRIPTION: A lean, medium-size brown snake with a vertical pupil. The color and markings are variable, and are location specific. Colors vary from yellowish to brown, with diamond-shaped or amorphous markings that may be faint or prominent. The Brown Tree Snake is venomous, with rear fangs, meaning the fangs are in the back of the jaw and not visible unless the mouth of the snake is open.

NATIVE DISTRIBUTION: It is native to eastern Indonesia, New Guinea, the Solomon Islands, and the coastal areas of northern and eastern Australia.

NORTH AMERICAN DISTRIBUTION: Appearances of this snake have been reported in North America, with specific reports from Alaska, Hawaii, Oklahoma, and Texas. No breeding populations have been reported in North America.

DATE(S) AND MEANS OF INTRODUCTION: Unknown.

THREATS: The Brown Tree Snake causes ecological devastation in the areas it invades. The snake was accidentally introduced into Guam in the 1940s in cargo carried to the island by the U.S. military. Guam is an island with no native snakes and no competitors. Brown Tree Snake populations have exploded, with several thousand snakes per square mile in the jungles of Guam. As an arboreal species, the Brown Tree Snake is exceptionally proficient at preying on birds. Over the past 70 years, the snakes have extirpated nearly all the native bird species in Guam and two of the three native bat species.

MANAGEMENT: The prevention of new infestations is critical. Islands with no native snakes are at a high risk of similar ecological impacts, should the Brown Tree Snake be introduced. A multitiered prevention and management program has been established for the Hawaiian Islands.

The plan includes systems to detect stowaway snakes in shipping cargo before it leaves port and before it is distributed to new locations. A highly trained "rapid response team" is deployed to eradicate any snakes that evade detection systems. Since the implementation of these systems in 1981, only eight snakes have been discovered and destroyed in Hawaii. New prevention and control strategies are regularly developed. Most recently, dogs trained to smell and hunt Brown Tree Snakes have been deployed in Hawaii.

Crocodylus niloticus

NILE CROCODILE

DESCRIPTION: The Nile Crocodile is the second-largest reptile in the world. It can reach up to 20 ft. (6 m) in length and weigh over 2,200 lbs. (1,000 kg). It is usually dark bronze on its back, becoming paler on the sides and belly, with various black spots and other markings.

NATIVE DISTRIBUTION: It is native to most of Africa, including Madagascar, in a variety of aquatic habitats.

NORTH AMERICAN DISTRIBUTION: So far, the Nile Crocodile is only reported in the Florida Everglades.

DATE(S) AND MEANS OF INTRODUCTION: The precise date and means of introduction are unknown. It was first reported in the Everglades in 2009. Some scientists speculate that these invasive crocodiles may have escaped from a nearby interactive zoo known as Predator World.

THREATS: The invasion of a new crocodile species in the Everglades will have significant ecological consequences for an already fragile habitat. The American crocodile native to this location is a threatened species, with fewer than 20,000 individuals left in the world. The Nile Crocodile may outcompete native crocodiles and potentially hybridize with native crocodiles. Hybrids could be larger and cause even greater disruption to the Everglade's ecosystem.

MANAGEMENT: The priority management strategy emphasizes the prevention of future Nile Crocodile invasions in this area. The U.S. Fish and Wildlife Service captured all known Nile Crocodiles from the Everglades and have a monitoring program in place to prevent future spread.

Python bivittatus

BURMESE PYTHON

DESCRIPTION: Large, robust constrictor type of snake, capable of attaining lengths of at least 20 ft. (6 m) and weighing close to 441 lbs. (200 kg). The snake's body is tannish in color, with brown splotches with a black border, a dark triangular patch on the top of the head, and a white stripe under the eye that extends to the corner of the mouth.

NATIVE DISTRIBUTION: It is native to much of southeast Asia, from southern China to India.

NORTH AMERICAN DISTRIBUTION: It is reported in South Florida and Puerto Rico.

DATE(S) AND MEANS OF INTRODUCTION: A precise date of introduction is not known, but it is believed to have been in the northern Everglades in the mid-1980s. It is thought that unwanted pets were released, which ultimately became established and invasive.

THREATS: There have been over 33 native species documented from the stomachs of Florida pythons, including birds, mammals, and alligators. The decline of several native species in the Everglades does correlate with the proliferation of the snake. Furthermore, it is believed to have also brought a lung parasite to Florida that is now infecting native species of snakes.

MANAGEMENT: Public awareness campaigns are designed to inform the public about the ecological impacts caused by the Burmese Python. It is illegal to possess or distribute the Burmese Python in Florida. They are illegal to import to the United States. Florida has established Exotic Pet Amnesty Days, where people can drop off their Burmese Pythons without repercussions. Eradication efforts include strategies such as baiting with poisoned mice and hunting.

Tupinambis teguixin

TEGU LIZARD, GOLDEN TEGU, BLACK TEGU, TIGER LIZARD

DESCRIPTION: A large, attractive lizard reaching up to 40 in. (1 m) long and weighing up to 9 lbs. (4 kg). The Tegu Lizard's markings can be variable, but it usually has brown and gold stripes along its entire body.

NATIVE DISTRIBUTION: The Tegu Lizard is native to South America.

NORTH AMERICAN DISTRIBUTION: Currently, there are breeding populations of the Tegu Lizard in some parts of South Florida.

DATE(S) AND MEANS OF INTRODUCTION: The invasive Tegu Lizard was most likely a released or escaped pet. The lizards were first reported as a breeding population in South Florida in 2016. Over 20,000 sightings have been reported since this time.

THREATS: The Tegu Lizard poses a significant threat to birds and other egg-laying species, such as the threatened American crocodile. It has few predators and reproduces rapidly.

MANAGEMENT: All Tegu Lizards have been added to the prohibited species list in Florida. This means all future sales of Tegu Lizards are prohibited in Florida, and all current pet owners must apply for an owner's permit, have their pets fitted with electronic tracking chips, and use approved cages to prevent escape.

Sturnus vulgaris

EUROPEAN STARLING

DESCRIPTION: A nondescript bird, up to 8¾ in. (22 cm) in length. It is primarily black, with an iridescent green or purple sheen. There may be white spots on the chest.

NATIVE DISTRIBUTION: It is native to a broad area from southwestern Asia to North Africa and Europe.

NORTH AMERICAN DISTRIBUTION: It is found throughout most of North America, from Canada to Central America and the Caribbean.

DATE(S) AND MEANS OF INTRODUCTION: Thirty pairs of starlings were introduced into New York City in 1890 by the American Acclimatization Society, which aimed to introduce native European flora and fauna to North America. One society member sought to populate North America with all the bird species mentioned in William Shakespeare's works, including the European Starling. The 60 European Starlings released in 1890 are the ancestors of most starlings found in North America today.

THREATS: They are flocking birds, often forming vast flocks, which can cause tremendous destruction to crop fields as they probe the ground, hunting for invertebrates. They are also considered a public nuisance by damaging homes and buildings and are known to carry several infectious disease–causing bacteria.

MANAGEMENT: Control strategies employed are either physical or chemical. Physical methods include sonic devices, antiperching structures, kites, hunting and trapping, and other tools to frighten off flocks. The physical control strategies are usually only temporary in their effectiveness. Chemical controls may be nonharmful repellents that activate pain receptors but are nonlethal or lethal options that kill large flocks and may have consequences for other wildlife.

MAMMALS

Felis catus

HOUSE CAT, FERAL CAT, COMMON CAT

DESCRIPTION: The ubiquitous House Cat is a small mammal, ranging from 6½ to 22 lbs. (3 to 10 kg) in weight and covered in fur of variable colors.

NATIVE DISTRIBUTION: As a domesticated species, the House Cat does not have a native range.

NORTH AMERICAN DISTRIBUTION: The House Cat is distributed across all of North America.

DATE(S) AND MEANS OF INTRODUCTION: The House Cat was probably not introduced into North America before the first European settlers. It was likely used as a pest deterrent on boats and later homesteads, and eventually became a companion animal.

THREATS: In North America, domesticated cats kill billions of birds and mammals annually. The International Union for Conservation of Nature (IUCN) has identified the domestic House Cat as one of the worst invasive species in the world, causing the extinction of at least 60 species of birds, reptiles, and mammals.

MANAGEMENT: In North America, domesticated House Cats fall into three major categories: indoor cats that rarely or never interact outdoors, cats that are primarily indoors but have free range to go outdoors, and feral domesticated cats that are always outdoors. It is estimated that at least 60 million of the 120 million cats in North America regularly go outdoors or are always outdoors. Keeping domestic cats indoors is the easiest and least expensive loss-prevention strategy. Because the domesticated cat is a beloved companion animal, strategies to manage feral populations are sometimes controversial. Some plans involve capture and euthanasia, and other strategies emphasize reproductive sterilization of feral cats, often referred to as "trap-neuter-release" programs.

Myocastor coypus

NUTRIA, COYPU

DESCRIPTION: A large rodent weighing about 11 lbs. (5 kg). It is found primarily in aquatic environments.

NATIVE DISTRIBUTION: It is native to South America.

NORTH AMERICAN DISTRIBUTION: Nutrias are found throughout most of North America, but populations in colder climates rapidly decline after frigid winters. The highest population densities are reported in warm, wet locations such as Louisiana.

DATE(S) AND MEANS OF INTRODUCTION: The precise date of introduction is unknown, but it was likely due to the fur industry in the late 19th or early 20th century. Nutrias are valued for their skin and fur.

THREATS: Nutrias are voracious eaters and can consume up to 20 percent of their body weight daily. The consumption of plant life surrounding aquatic areas has resulted in shifting wetlands from marshes and swamps to open water, the habitat for wetland species and negatively impacting the essential protection from floods that is provided by marches and other wetlands. Nutrias may also carry zoonotic pathogens and parasites.

MANAGEMENT: The primary control strategy used is eradication through trapping. When Nutria fur prices are high, the Nutria populations are better controlled, and a correlating reduction in the loss of wetland habitats is observed. Nutria meat is also edible, and some educational campaigns have emphasized the ethical side of trapping Nutrias for their leather and meat.

Rattus rattus

HOUSE RAT, BLACK RAT

DESCRIPTION: A small to medium-size rodent reaching about 10 in. (25 cm) in length and weighing up to 500 g.

NATIVE DISTRIBUTION: The House Rat is native to India.

NORTH AMERICAN DISTRIBUTION: It is spread across the entire North American continent, with the largest populations in cities and other areas with high levels of human activity.

DATE(S) AND MEANS OF INTRODUCTION: The House Rat was most likely brought on ships from Europe to North America in the 17th century or earlier.

THREATS: Rats demonstrate all of the characteristics of an invasive species that is likely to cause a harmful impact on an ecosystem. They reproduce and grow rapidly, and they are highly intelligent and quick to adapt. The House Rat has caused the extinction of dozens of species and the death of millions or even billions of humans over the course of history. Part of their adaptability is their flexible diet. Rats will eat almost anything, including each other. Their voracious eating has contributed to the extinction of birds, small mammals, reptiles, and even plants. When introduced into an island habit, rats are especially harmful. In Hawaii, the House Rat is responsible for critically endangering over 80 species, mostly birds, due to predation. The House Rat also carries several human pathogens, often disseminated in rat urine. The House Rat is famously known for spreading the bubonic plague (*Yersinia pestis*) in association with fleas, killing as much as one-third of the human population at the time of the plagues!

MANAGEMENT: House Rat population management is most critical on islands or similar locations where they can cause the most ecological harm. Standard trapping and baiting with toxic chemicals are employed, but the most promising research is focused on chemical sterilization that would ultimately work to eliminate rats from island habitats.

Sus scrofa

WILD PIG

DESCRIPTION: The Wild Pig is a medium-size pig descended from domesticated pigs or wild boar hybrids. They tend to be somewhat hairier than domestic pigs and may have a mane, depending on the presence of wild boar ancestry. Colors are usually black but may be white, brown, gray, or mixtures of two or more of those colors.

NATIVE DISTRIBUTION: They are native to a large portion of Europe, Asia, and North Africa, although the current range of the species has been significantly reduced. They have been spread nearly throughout the world.

NORTH AMERICAN DISTRIBUTION: They are found throughout a large portion of North America, absent only from parts that are especially dry or cold. In warm climates, they need wet, muddy areas for wallowing, and snow significantly impacts their ability to move and find food.

DATE(S) AND MEANS OF INTRODUCTION: Christopher Columbus brought pigs to the West Indies in 1493, and Hernando de Soto brought pigs to the Gulf Coast in 1539. They may have been introduced into Hawaii by Polynesians approximately 1,000 years ago.

THREATS: They significantly impact agricultural and natural areas, causing widespread soil disruption and reduction of native species, ultimately causing crop losses, reduced biodiversity, and localized extinctions. They are also known to carry diseases that affect both humans and livestock. They are adaptable to many types of habitats and can have high reproduction rates in favorable areas.

MANAGEMENT: The most effective means of controlling or eradicating Wild Pig populations is using a combination of hunting and poisoning. Pigs may be shot through hunting endeavors or from helicopters. Poisoning is usually through baits, although they are not selective, and other animals will likely feed on them also.

PLANTS

Alliaria petiolata

GARLIC MUSTARD

DESCRIPTION: A biennial or short-lived perennial plant in the mustard family. During its first year, it forms a rosette of round basal leaves with a crinkly-appearing surface. During the spring of its second year, it sends up flowering stalks bearing white, four-petaled flowers. All parts of the plant emit a garlic-like odor, especially noticeable when crushed.

NATIVE DISTRIBUTION: It is native to China, Western Europe, and North Africa.

NORTH AMERICAN DISTRIBUTION: It is currently found in most, if not all, states and Canadian provinces, primarily a denizen of forested or otherwise somewhat shady habitats.

DATE(S) AND MEANS OF INTRODUCTION: It was first discovered on Long Island, New York, in 1868. Over the next few decades, it slowly spread, until the mid-1900s, when it quickly reached most states and Canadian provinces. It was not identified as a threatening invasive species until the late 1980s. It was likely brought to North America for culinary and medicinal purposes.

THREATS: It can form dense patches of vegetation, effectively smothering and displacing native vegetation. Furthermore, it is a host of several plant-pathogenic viruses. It can quickly and voraciously infest new locations and is easily spread through human activities. Several native butterfly species have been known to use it as an alternative host, but studies have shown caterpillars that hatch on Garlic Mustard are unlikely to survive to adulthood.

MANAGEMENT: Due to the production of a copious dormant seed bank, any management plan developed for Garlic Mustard should be implemented for a minimum of three years to ensure the plant does not reinfest a treated location. Eradication methods should be employed before seed set has occurred. Hand-pulling and mowing to ground level are both effective strategies and can be used alone or in combination with herbicide applications.

Ailanthus altissima

TREE OF HEAVEN

DESCRIPTION: A small to medium-size deciduous tree with graceful arching branches and large, pinnately compound leaves. The common name, "Tree of Heaven," refers to the tree's ability to grow quickly upward toward the heavens. The flowers are small and yellow and produce a samara fruit.

NATIVE DISTRIBUTION: This species is native to northern and central China.

NORTH AMERICAN DISTRIBUTION: The Tree of Heaven is found throughout all of North America. It has been identified as an invasive species in at least 10 states and three Canadian provinces.

DATE(S) AND MEANS OF INTRODUCTION: It was first introduced into North America in 1794 for its beautiful form, fast growth, and resistance to most pests.

THREATS: The Tree of Heaven reproduces quickly and has a rapid growth rate. When it escapes cultivation, it produces thickets of dense monoculture. It shades out the understory and reduces the habitat for native species. The presence of the Tree of Heaven in a habitat is correlated with reduced species biodiversity. Several species have become endangered as a direct result of the Tree of Heaven entering the ecosystem.

MANAGEMENT: One reason the Tree of Heaven has become so invasive is the great difficulty encountered when trying to remove an established tree. Seedlings should be pulled, using care to ensure the entire taproot is removed, or new sprouts will emerge. Older trees should be cut down, and the herbicide triclopyr should be applied to the cut stem. Trunks should be regularly monitored for new sprouts.

Ardisia crenata

CORAL ARDISIA

DESCRIPTION: A multistemmed evergreen shrub, up to 59 in. (1.5 m) in height. Its leaves are up to 8 in. (20 cm) long and dark green in color, with a waxy appearance and scalloped margins. Small pink or white flowers are borne in axillary clusters.

NATIVE DISTRIBUTION: It is native to Southeast Asia, from Korea to India.

NORTH AMERICAN DISTRIBUTION: The Coral Ardisia is currently found in eight states, primarily the southern states, as well as Hawaii, Missouri, and Puerto Rico.

DATE(S) AND MEANS OF INTRODUCTION: It was first brought to North America (Florida) as an imported ornamental plant in the early 1900s. It was introduced into Hawaii in 1930.

THREATS: It can form very dense patches in the understory of forests, effectively shading out native species.

MANAGEMENT: The management of Coral Ardisia should include preventing new plantings in the landscape by regulating commerce and transport in tropical and subtropical locations where this plant is hardy. Existing landscape plants should be removed. Small seedlings can be hand-pulled, mowed, or burned. Larger shrubs should be cut and observed for regrowth.

Azolla pinnata

FEATHERED MOSQUITO FERN

DESCRIPTION: A small, floating aquatic fern, up to 1 in. (2.5 cm) long, with feathery, triangular fronds composed of minute, overlapping scales. Leaves are often tinted red, giving infested areas an overall reddish appearance from a distance. It favors bodies of water with little to no wave action.

NATIVE DISTRIBUTION: This fern is widely distributed from Africa to Southeast Asia, China, Japan, New Guinea, and Australia.

NORTH AMERICAN DISTRIBUTION: It is confined mainly to Florida due to climatic reasons. It is reportedly unable to survive at temperatures below 39°F (4°C).

DATE(S) AND MEANS OF INTRODUCTION: It was first reported in Florida in 2002 and most likely arrived through the aquarium trade.

THREATS: This species can form dense surface mats, which not only shades out native submerged species but reduces the concentration of dissolved oxygen in and around the mats. Other impacts include interfering with fishing, boating, and other aquatic activities.

MANAGEMENT: New infestations are prevented by regulations in place preventing the sale and transport of *Azolla pinnata*; however, regulations are not strictly enforced. The Azolla weevil (*Stenopelmus rufinasus*) eats *Azolla* and has been employed as a biocontrol organism. Some research has shown using surface skimmers to collect plant material from the water to be effective, but this method is not yet widely employed. Chemical applications, including the herbicides diquat, glyphosate, and terbutryn, are effective but pollute the water supply.

Caulerpa taxifolia

INVASIVE SEAWEED, KILLER ALGAE

DESCRIPTION: This species is an aquatic macroalga that produces a long, horizontal stolon (runner) in the sediment. Frond-like filaments that have been compared to the leaves of the yew (*Taxus*) extend from the stolons.

NATIVE DISTRIBUTION: This species is native to warmer, tropical waters and is found primarily in the Caribbean, Maldives, parts of the East African coast, Hawaii, Fiji, and tropical Australia.

NORTH AMERICAN DISTRIBUTION: It has colonized small regions of the coast in Southern California.

DATE(S) AND MEANS OF INTRODUCTION: Naturally occurring populations are not invasive. A strain selected for its ability to grow in colder waters by the aquarium managers for a German zoo was accidentally released and displaced native algae. The cold-hardy "aquarium strain" can survive out of water and can grow on different surfaces. Invasive Seaweed was first reported in California in 1997.

THREATS: The aquarium strain outcompetes native *Caulerpa taxifolia* and other native alga species. It produces toxic metabolites, most abundantly caulerpenyne, that render the alga inedible and can kill or deter some native species, although it is not harmful to humans.

MANAGEMENT: California has banned the sale or transport of the aquarium strain of *C. taxifolia* to prevent its spread to new locations. Eradication is exceptionally challenging because the alga reproduces by fragmentation. If a piece is broken, the fragments can grow into new populations. The only effective eradication strategies involve applying chemicals that kill everything in the water. After a nearly decade-long effort that cost over $7 million, the aquarium strain has been eradicated from coastal California, but the problem persists in the Mediterranean.

Centaurea stoebe

SPOTTED KNAPWEED

DESCRIPTION: Spotted Knapweed is a perennial reaching 40 to 80 in. (1 to 2 m) in height. It has grayish-green leaves and small purple composite flowers. Each plant produces thousands of seeds that can survive for up to a decade. The roots secrete allelopathic chemicals that inhibit the growth of other plant species. Spotted Knapweed populations are often observed growing in a monoculture because grazing animals typically will not eat this plant.

NATIVE DISTRIBUTION: Spotted Knapweed is native to Bulgaria, Hungary, Romania, Ukraine, and Russia.

NORTH AMERICAN DISTRIBUTION: In North America, Spotted Knapweed is found in every U.S. state and nine Canadian provinces.

DATE(S) AND MEANS OF INTRODUCTION: It was most likely introduced into North America in contaminated alfalfa seed in the late 19th century.

THREATS: Spotted Knapweed produces high quantities of seed and establishes large populations quickly. It limits the growth of plants growing nearby by producing allelopathic chemicals. It causes a loss of biodiversity, and it degrades the quality of forage land.

MANAGEMENT: Seed sources for prairies and cover crops should be of high quality and carefully screened to ensure they are free from contamination with Spotted Knapweed seed. Manual removal of plants in small areas can effectively reduce Spotted Knapweed populations, but care should be taken to only remove plants before they have produced seed; otherwise, there is a risk of spreading seeds to new locations. Knapweed in larger areas can be controlled by mowing right before seed formation occurs. Herbicide applications can be effective, but they are costly and not a long-term solution.

Conium maculatum

POISON HEMLOCK

DESCRIPTION: Poison Hemlock is a biennial herb that reaches about 10 ft. (3 m) tall. The thick stem is hollow, hairless, and covered with purple streaks; these features are useful in helping to distinguish this genus from other similar genera in the carrot family but should not be used as a definitive identifying characteristic. Extreme caution should be used with this plant. Poison Hemlock is frequently misidentified as one of various nontoxic, edible plants in the carrot family, resulting in sometimes fatal consequences.

NATIVE DISTRIBUTION: It is native to Europe, North Africa, and tropical regions of Asia.

NORTH AMERICAN DISTRIBUTION: It is distributed globally and is a noxious weed found throughout North America.

DATE(S) AND MEANS OF INTRODUCTION: Poison Hemlock was first reported in North America in the 1890s, but no mechanism of introduction is known. It is speculated that this species was accidentally spread in grain shipments from Europe.

THREATS: Poison Hemlock is a highly toxic plant that has killed humans and is a significant contributor to livestock losses, with estimated losses exceeding $300 million annually. In addition to being a serious threat to human and animal health and safety, Poison Hemlock is an aggressive plant that outcompetes native species and significantly modifies the ecosystem where it becomes established.

MANAGEMENT: Poison Hemlock has been designated a noxious weed in 11 U.S. states, as well as Guatemala, Honduras, Mexico, and Costa Rica. Management of Poison Hemlock is most important when land is used for animal grazing. Under these circumstances, poisonous plant populations should be carefully monitored and controlled. The most effective strategy for eradicating Poison Hemlock is physical removal of seedlings (wearing gloves), mowing older plants, and judicious application of chemical herbicides.

Cynodon dactylon

BERMUDA GRASS

DESCRIPTION: Bermuda Grass is a short perennial rhizomatous and stoloniferous grass. It has horizontally spreading stolons (runners) that root about every 4 in. (10 cm) along the stem, where leaves and flower stems are produced. The leaves stick out at a 90° angle from the stolon and are narrowly lanceolate, from ²/₅ to 6 in. (1 to 15 cm) long. Eventually, the grass forms a dense mat of stems and leaves. The inflorescence is a whorl of racemes at the end of the flower stalk, which can be up to 10 in. (25 cm) tall.

NATIVE DISTRIBUTION: It is believed to be native to Africa.

NORTH AMERICAN DISTRIBUTION: It is widely distributed, from Central America and the Caribbean to the northern United States, with a few occurrences in far southern Canada. It apparently is only absent from three U.S. states: Alaska and the Dakotas.

DATE(S) AND MEANS OF INTRODUCTION: In the United States, it was first introduced in 1807. It is a popular turf grass for athletic fields, golf courses, and lawns.

THREATS: Considered the second-worst weed in the world, it is a very fast-growing, mat-forming grass that can quickly overtake the area it is planted in. It is also drought, flood, and fire tolerant. It becomes especially vigorous and dominant in crop fields, and is particularly noxious in sugarcane, cotton, rice, and tobacco fields. When established, it aggressively competes for resources with crop plants, and can cause significant yield decreases. It is also an alternate host of several agricultural diseases and pests, and can be poisonous to grazing livestock.

MANAGEMENT: A commonly employed strategy for control and eradication is to plow the infestation, then follow up with an herbicide treatment. This method is effective and relatively inexpensive. Soil solarization has also been found to be an effective means of controlling this plant. Other strategies include planting cover crops that are able to shade out the grass, or increasing the density of crop plantings.

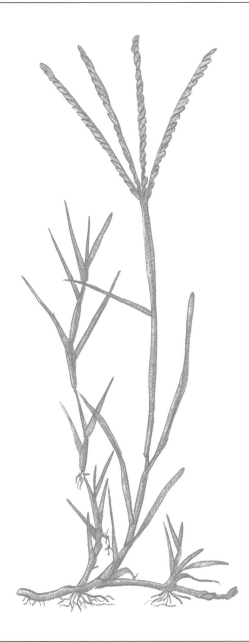

Cytisus scoparius

SCOTCH BROOM

DESCRIPTION: A deciduous shrub in the pea family that usually has a dense mass of erect stems. The flowers are yellow and pealike, and the fruit is a brownish-black pod.

NATIVE DISTRIBUTION: It is native to most of Western Europe, with scattered native populations in Eastern Europe.

NORTH AMERICAN DISTRIBUTION: It is distributed across North America and has an invasive status in at least 30 U.S. states and four Canadian provinces.

DATE(S) AND MEANS OF INTRODUCTION: It was introduced into North America in the mid-19th century, possibly carried in ships as ballast and dumped upon arrival. Several close insect and disease associates of Scotch Broom were reported in North America concurrently, which provides additional evidence to confirm the origin from ballast.

THREATS: Outside of its natural range, Scotch Broom grows in dense thickets. It produces chemicals that inhibit the growth of other plant species and can establish a large monoculture. This has directly reduced the populations of at least 30 plant species, which likely correlates with a significant loss of pollinating insect species. The thickets also create a fire hazard and reduce the value of rangeland.

MANAGEMENT: New infestations can be reduced by eliminating soil movement from infested locations to new locations. Good sanitation practices, like cleaning boots before entering new locations, help to eliminate soil movement. An integrated management plan, including herbicide application, hand-pulling, and burning, is the most effective approach to controlling established Scotch Broom populations. Triclopyr is the most effective selective herbicide for Scotch Broom and can be applied after leaves have fully emerged. Hand-pulling young plants tends to encourage seed germination from the soil seed bank, but combined with annual burns in early spring, this multiyear management approach can control Scotch Broom.

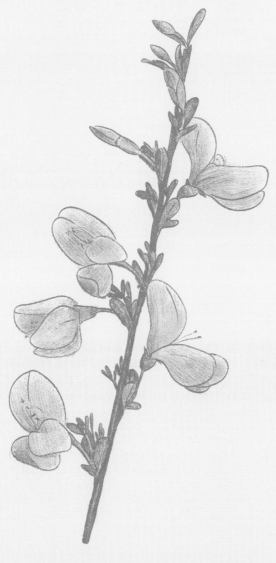

Euonymus alatus

BURNING BUSH, WINGED SPINDLE

DESCRIPTION: A medium-size shrub with uniquely square-shaped branches. Branches have sharp ridges or "wings." In the fall, its leaves and stems turn bright red, hence the common name "Burning Bush."

NATIVE DISTRIBUTION: It is native to northeastern Asia.

NORTH AMERICAN DISTRIBUTION: As a popular ornamental, it is widespread throughout North America. Naturalized populations are reported throughout the Midwest and eastern half of the United States.

DATE(S) AND MEANS OF INTRODUCTION: It was first introduced into North America in the late 19th century for use as a landscape ornamental. It is frequently used in both residential and municipal applications.

THREATS: Burning Bush produces copious amounts of seed and quickly outcompetes native plant species, reducing forest biodiversity and altering food webs.

MANAGEMENT: A key to prevention is reducing seed sources. Due to the popularity of this species as a landscape ornamental, educating homeowners about the invasive qualities of Burning Bush is part of a prevention strategy. Eradication is achieved through the physical removal of shrubs, emphasizing the reduction of primary seed sources. After removal, stumps can be treated with glyphosate to inhibit regrowth.

Euphorbia virgata (formerly *Euphorbia esula*)

LEAFY SPURGE

DESCRIPTION: An herbaceous perennial up to 35 in. (90 cm) in height. Leaves are alternate and very long and narrow, up to 3½ x ½ in. (90 x 12 mm). Terminal flowers are borne in a flat or rounded cluster on multiple stems that all emerge from the stem tip. Individual flowers are small and lack petals; however, they are enveloped by two yellowish, round bracts (modified leaves that resemble petals).

NATIVE DISTRIBUTION: It is native to temperate areas of Europe and Asia.

NORTH AMERICAN DISTRIBUTION: It is present in all of the states north of a line from Virginia to Oregon, and in adjacent parts of Canada. There are a few isolated occurrences outside of this area, in Mexico and the southwestern United States.

DATE(S) AND MEANS OF INTRODUCTION: It was first seen in Massachusetts in 1827, most likely arriving in the soil ballast of cargo ships from Europe. Populations in the north-central and western United States are likely descended from two other separate incidents of introduction.

THREATS: This is one of the worst invasive plants in North America, in terms of the ecological and economical impact it has, as well as how difficult it is to eradicate. It has multiple adaptations that have allowed it to become such a problem. For starters, it has a deep taproot (up to 2 m), as well as an extensive lateral root system, which gives the plant a substantial nutrient reserve and the ability to withstand droughts. As the lateral roots spread, they also send up new shoots. It also emerges, and its seeds germinate, very early in the spring, giving the plant a competitive head start relative to native species. The roots are also able to secrete out chemicals that are sprayed on the plant, such as herbicides. It produces a very large number of seeds that can be dispersed over great distances and remain viable for at least eight years. The plant also has a milky sap that is toxic to animals, so most grazers do not touch this plant. And, finally, it also produces a substance in the soil that inhibits the growth of other species. Altogether, this makes for a very successful invasive species, one that is able to efficiently outcompete and displace native vegetation, while requiring significant effort to control or eradicate.

MANAGEMENT: Various methods are employed in attempts to control and eradicate this species. As mentioned above, herbicides may be ineffectual, but not entirely, and are often used, especially on very large, dense colonies. Cultivation or mowing of patches twice a year has shown to be successful, although it takes several years of doing that to have a significant impact. Despite the toxic sap, sheep and goats will graze this species. This, along with prescribed burns, can be used to control vegetative growth when available. There are certain grass species that can be planted that are able to compete with Leafy Spurge and limit its spread. The most effective method, however, is the use of biocontrol agents: several insect species have been identified and introduced that do have an impact on Leafy Spurge.

Heracleum mantegazzianum

GIANT HOGWEED

DESCRIPTION: A large, robust monocarpic (meaning it dies after flowering and producing seeds) perennial plant in the carrot family. Leaves are typically coarsely lobed with toothed margins and can attain tremendous sizes, up to 10 ft. (3 m) long and 80 in. (2 m) wide. At 3 to 5 years of age, it sends up a flowering stalk up to 16½ ft. (5 m) high and 4 in. (10 cm) in diameter. The stem has ridges and purple blotches and is covered by bristles. Flowers are terminal compound umbels bearing numerous small white flowers. The entire umbel can approach 40 in. (1 m) in diameter.

NATIVE DISTRIBUTION: It is native to Southern Russia and Georgia.

NORTH AMERICAN DISTRIBUTION: In North America, it is found in at least 14 U.S. states, all east of the Mississippi River or in the Pacific Northwest. It is also found in British Columbia and the Canadian provinces from Ontario eastward.

DATE(S) AND MEANS OF INTRODUCTION: It appears to have been introduced into North America at some point in the mid-1900s, with the earliest reports from Ontario and Washington state. The primary cause of its spread is its use as a garden ornamental, due to its large size.

THREATS: It can outcompete and displace most of the plants in an area, other than trees, due to the shading effects of its large leaves. This ultimately leaves areas of bare soil in infested areas, which are then more prone to erosion. The bristles found on the plant contain chemicals that can result in photodermatitis on the skin of humans. Such cases of dermatitis can become quite severe, producing oozing blisters and/or actual skin burns.

MANAGEMENT: An integrated pest management (IPM) system is most effective for controlling Giant Hogweed. Heavy grazing has been shown to reduce populations. A combination of hand-pulling young plants (gloves should be worn), digging up large plants, and applying the herbicide glyphosate has effectively treated locations over a multiyear period.

Hydrilla verticillata

WATER THYME

DESCRIPTION: A submerged aquatic plant that forms long, branching stems up to 10 ft. (3 m) long. Leaves are linearly lanceolate, up to 1½ in. (40 mm) long, and are in whorls of 3 to 12. Spines are found on the lower surface of the leaves. In overall appearance, it resembles *Elodea* (waterweeds). Flowers are three parted, tiny, and inconspicuous.

NATIVE DISTRIBUTION: It is believed to be native to a broad swath of land, from Africa to East Asia.

NORTH AMERICAN DISTRIBUTION: It is found in at least 35 U.S. states, with the highest populations occurring in a band from Massachusetts to Mexico, including Florida. It is also present on several Caribbean islands.

DATE(S) AND MEANS OF INTRODUCTION: It was first imported into Missouri in 1947 for aquatic ornamental plant purposes.

THREATS: It can form large, dense masses at all depths of the water column. In turn, this shades out and displaces many native species. It is also economically devastating, as it damages hydroelectric dams and fisheries. Costs associated with *Hydrilla* mitigation in the United States are in the hundreds of millions of dollars annually.

MANAGEMENT: Managing Water Thyme infestations is very costly and challenging. Chemical control is temporarily effective but pollutes the water and surrounding wildlife. *Hydrilla* also acquires resistance to herbicides over time. In Florida, where *Hydrilla* is a serious problem, herbicide-resistant *Hydrilla* has populated several large bodies of water. Physical removal is also costly, but some advances have been made through the engineering of specially designed equipment to harvest *Hydrilla* from the water. The most promising management strategy may be the use of biocontrol organisms, like the grass carp (*Ctenopharyngodon idella*), which feeds on *Hydrilla*.

Hygrophila polysperma

INDIAN SWAMPWEED, EAST INDIAN HYGROPHILA

DESCRIPTION: A rhizomatous aquatic perennial plant that forms dense stands. Plants are mostly submerged and rooted in the substrate, although some are free-floating. The leaves are oblong and up to $3^1/_6$ in. (8 cm) long. Flowers are small, bluish white, and often hidden by stem leaves.

NATIVE DISTRIBUTION: It is native to tropical parts of Asia in various wet habitats.

NORTH AMERICAN DISTRIBUTION: In North America, it is present in Mexico and the southeastern United States, from Virginia to Texas.

DATE(S) AND MEANS OF INTRODUCTION: In 1945, it was first imported to the United States through the aquarium trade. The first report of naturalization occurred in 1965 in Tampa, Florida, and it reached Texas by 1969.

THREATS: It is a popular aquarium plant, facilitating this species' spread. It has a vigorous growth rate (it can cover up to 10 acres per year) and quickly becomes the dominant plant species under favorable conditions. The robust growth shades out native species, reducing their abundance and the organisms that depend on them. They can propagate vegetatively from fragments, and early eradication attempts, including mowing, resulted in higher plant populations.

MANAGEMENT: Significant efforts are being focused on preventing the spread of the species from places it has naturalized. These strategies include the early detection and eradication of new occurrences, public awareness and education about this species, requiring the cleaning of boats as they leave a body of water, and banning or restricting the commerce of Indian Swampweed. It is difficult and costly to control this species with herbicides.

Kali tragus

TUMBLEWEED, SALTWORT, RUSSIAN THISTLE

DESCRIPTION: An annual forb, up to 40 in. (1 m) tall and forming a round, tangled clump of stems that eventually dies and breaks off, forming a tumbleweed. Leaves are small and leathery, with a very sharp spine at the tip.

NATIVE DISTRIBUTION: It is native to a large portion of Europe, from Russia to the United Kingdom and down to Portugal.

NORTH AMERICAN DISTRIBUTION: It is found from Canada to southern Mexico. In the United States, it is present in most states outside of the southeastern part of the country.

DATE(S) AND MEANS OF INTRODUCTION: It was first reported from South Dakota in the late 1800s. It was in flaxseed brought by Russian immigrants.

THREATS: It can outcompete and displace native vegetation. Its tumbleweed ability allows it to quickly spread and colonize an area. During productive years, Tumbleweeds can congregate in surprisingly large masses, covering automobiles and damaging fences. The dried tumbles are highly flammable and present a fire risk. Some people have reported allergic reactions to the plant, either from simply handling the plant, or by breathing in its pollen.

MANAGEMENT: Some herbicides are effective on Tumbleweeds; however, damage to crops needs to be considered when applying. Hand-pulling and mowing can be effective in small areas, but is just not feasible over large areas. Reducing the grazing pressure in an infested area has also shown to be an effective means of control.

Ligustrum japonicum

JAPANESE PRIVET

DESCRIPTION: Japanese Privet is a large evergreen shrub or small tree, growing up to 20 ft. (6 m) tall.

NATIVE DISTRIBUTION: It is native to Japan and South Korea.

NORTH AMERICAN DISTRIBUTION: It is primarily found in the southeastern United States, where it has escaped cultivation.

DATE(S) AND MEANS OF INTRODUCTION: Precise introduction dates are uncertain. As early as 1794, it was introduced into the American South as a hedgerow and landscape plant.

THREATS: When it escapes from cultivation, Japanese Privet forms dense thickets that shade out the understory plants and alter the habitat for native birds and mammals. It is challenging to remove well-established shrubs. This species produces numerous seeds that are disseminated by birds, which aids in spreading the invasive species to new locations and reinfesting treated sites.

MANAGEMENT: Not using this species in the landscape is the most effective prevention strategy. All landscape specimens should be removed, but removal should not occur when Japanese Privet is fruiting, to reduce the risk of spreading seeds to new locations. Chemical control combined with manual removal is an effective strategy for heavily populated areas. It is often a multiyear effort to completely treat an infested site.

Lonicera morrowii

HONEYSUCKLE

DESCRIPTION: A deciduous woody shrub with hollow stems, up to 8 ft. (2.5 m) in height. Leaves are simple, elliptical in shape, and up to 2 in. (50 mm) long. Flowers are bilaterally symmetrical, delicate in appearance, and colored white, aging to yellow. Flower stalks, sepals (structures that surround the petals of a flower bud), and petals are conspicuously hairy. The fruits are red or yellow fleshy berries, about $^1/_5$ in. (0.5 cm) in diameter.

NATIVE DISTRIBUTION: This species is native to Japan, China, and the Korean Peninsula.

NORTH AMERICAN DISTRIBUTION: The Honeysuckle is native to the eastern part of North America, from Minnesota to Nova Scotia, south to the Great Smoky Mountains.

DATE(S) AND MEANS OF INTRODUCTION: It was first introduced into the United States in Massachusetts in 1862. It was then widely planted as an ornamental landscape shrub.

THREATS: Honeysuckle tends to invade disturbed forest habitats, quickly becoming the dominant understory species. This negatively impacts native plant species in the area, restricting their growth and development, primarily due to shading effects, in many cases creating nothing but bare ground underneath it. This is exacerbated by its ability to leaf out earlier in the spring than native species, as well as retaining foliage later into the fall than native species. It also hybridizes with another non-native honeysuckle (*L. tatarica*), the offspring of which may be even more invasive than either parent species.

MANAGEMENT: Because of this species' tendency to leaf out very early in the spring, this is a good time to begin eradication attempts. Small seedlings can be hand-pulled, and larger shrubs can be cut down or tugged out (using tools and/or machinery). Herbicides like glyphosate can be applied to stems.

Lygodium microphyllum

OLD WORLD CLIMBING FERN

DESCRIPTION: Old World Climbing Ferns (OWCFs) are true ferns composed of long, vining fronds that can reach over 98 ft. (30 m) long and grow vertically and horizontally, eventually forming dense mats of vegetation. The rachis (stem) is green to reddish brown. The attached branches (pinnae) have pairs of either vegetative or fertile leaves (pinnules). Leaflets are oblong and slightly lobed. Reproductive structures called sori surround the edges of fertile leaves. Underground stems (rhizomes) are wiry, thin, and brown to black. Rhizomes may also form dense mats of vegetation on the ground.

NATIVE DISTRIBUTION: As reflected in its common name, OWCF has a vast native range, including large areas of Asia, Africa, Europe, and Australia.

NORTH AMERICAN DISTRIBUTION: OWCF is currently only reported in Florida.

DATE(S) AND MEANS OF INTRODUCTION: It was brought to the United States as a cultivated plant and quickly escaped cultivation. The University of Florida Herbarium collections include a specimen from a cultivated OWCF plant observed at a Delray Beach nursery in 1958 that is the earliest recorded observation of OWCF in the United States. By 1960, it was observed and collected in the wild, and by the early 1990s, it had become an established invasive species in South Florida.

THREATS: Numerous invasive species threaten the ecology of the Florida Everglades, and OWCF has become one of the most destructive invaders of this region in the past 30 years. This invader is estimated to cover more than 2 million acres of the South Florida habitat, including many ecosystems that support rare and endangered species. The long vining fronds rapidly engulf large areas of vegetation and grow up, over, and within canopy trees. The invasive vegetation creates large, thick, horizontal mats within the canopy. These mats smother trees and shade the understory vegetation. Dead vegetation encircles infested trees from top to bottom, creating a fuel source for forest fires that would have otherwise been contained to the ground. Mats can also form in the swampy wetlands, many of which serve as the headwaters of major rivers in South Florida, posing a severe risk to water quality.

MANAGEMENT: A rigorous prevention program is in place, including regulating the possession, propagation, sale, and transport of OWCF at both the state and federal levels. Controlling infestations has proven to be very challenging, labor intensive, and costly, with research to identify effective control strategies beginning over 40 years ago. The only consistently effective treatment involves the application of herbicides containing the active ingredients glyphosate, triclopyr, and metsulfuron. Effective control requires multiple applications on infested locations annually for at least two years. Management plans include strategies for applying the herbicides as aerial applications over large areas and a combination of backpack spraying and "poodle cut"—a technique that involves cutting fronds at waist height and applying herbicides with a backpack sprayer. Foliage-eating moths and mites are possible biocontrol agents, but there is currently no effective biocontrol strategy.

Lythrum salicaria

PURPLE LOOSESTRIFE

DESCRIPTION: An attractive wetland perennial reaching about 6½ ft. (2 m) tall. It produces showy purple flowers on long stems in summer to late summer. Fruits are capsules that can contain up to 1,000,000 seeds per plant.

NATIVE DISTRIBUTION: This species is native to Europe and parts of Asia and Africa.

NORTH AMERICAN DISTRIBUTION: Purple Loosestrife is distributed across North America and is considered invasive in over 30 U.S. states and two Canadian provinces.

DATE(S) AND MEANS OF INTRODUCTION: The first recorded North American observation was on the east coast in 1814. It is speculated that the seeds were brought over unintentionally in sheep's wool or shipping ballast.

THREATS: This species has a rapid reproduction rate and quickly produces vast monocultures in wetlands. Purple Loosestrife drastically alters many aspects of wetland ecology, including reducing water flow rates, increasing eutrophication, and disturbing soil nitrogen cycling. It has a direct economic impact by reducing the value and quality of livestock grazing land and decreasing the nutritional quality of hay produced from meadows where Purple Loosestrife grows in monoculture. It may directly result in the loss of livestock by reducing water availability at irrigation sites. The impact on native species' biodiversity is unclear.

MANAGEMENT: Despite regulations limiting the sale and transport of Purple Loosestrife, this species is still readily available to purchase as an ornamental landscape plant. The first step in prevention is eliminating cultivated Purple Loosestrife sales. These cultivated varieties are often marketed as sterile, but they reproduce vegetatively, and studies suggest they regain the ability to reproduce sexually over generations.

Even after multiple years, manual removal and mowing do not effectively reduce population density. Attempts to use three different insect species that eat Purple Loosestrife as biocontrol agents also failed and, in fact, seemed to impact several native plant species more than Purple Loosestrife. Spot use of herbicides, especially glyphosate, is currently the most effective management option.

Miconia calvescens

VELVET TREE, BUSH CURRANT, MICONIA

DESCRIPTION: A small tree with a maximum height of 52½ ft. (16 m). It has very large leaves—up to 35½ in. (90 cm) long and 12 in. (30 cm) wide. The leaves are dark green, sometimes with a purple tinge, and elliptical in shape, and have a very prominent leaf venation in a herringbone-like pattern. Flowers are borne in panicles up to 12 in. (30 cm) long. They are small, with five white or pink petals. The fruits are small (0.5 cm), dark-purple globose berries.

NATIVE DISTRIBUTION: Its native range is from Mexico to Argentina.

NORTH AMERICAN DISTRIBUTION: In North America, it is found (as an invasive species) in some Caribbean islands and Hawaii.

DATE(S) AND MEANS OF INTRODUCTION: It was introduced into Hawaii sometime around the early 1960s. A form with bicolored leaves was discovered in Mexico in the 1930s, which became a very popular ornamental plant in greenhouses and tropical areas.

THREATS: In Hawaii, it is considered the worst invasive plant species. It is able to form dense monocultures. Because of the large size of its leaves, it completely shades out the ground underneath, eliminating plants growing under it. It also has a very shallow root system that makes the ground more susceptible to erosion, and there have been landslides in Hawaii that have been attributed to this tree. The fruit is very well-liked by many bird species, facilitating widespread dispersal of the seeds, and the tree can flower and set fruit multiple times per year.

MANAGEMENT: Quarantine regulations are in place in many countries, in hopes of preventing further infestations. Public information campaigns are active in many of these same countries. In most places, a combination of manual pulling/cutting of trees, followed by an herbicide application, has proven to be somewhat effective. Proper sanitation of clothing and equipment after working in areas with this tree is also used to prevent any unintentional seed dispersal. It is believed that biological control, ultimately, will be the most effective solution, and research studies on a number of different insects are currently underway.

Myriophyllum spicatum

EURASIAN WATERMILFOIL

DESCRIPTION: A perennial, rhizomatous submerged aquatic plant up to 98½ in. (250 cm) in length. Leaves are feather-like and in whorls of four. Spikes of inconspicuous, whorled flowers emerge above the water's surface. It is found in water at a depth of up to 10 ft. (3 m).

NATIVE DISTRIBUTION: It is native to Europe and parts of Asia and Africa.

NORTH AMERICAN DISTRIBUTION: Found throughout nearly all of North America, from southern Canada to central Mexico.

DATE(S) AND MEANS OF INTRODUCTION: Actual dates and means of introduction are unknown, but it was likely first brought to America in the 1940s to be used as an aquarium plant. It was present in Canada by the 1970s. Localized spread is facilitated by transporting plant fragments between bodies of water, such as on a boat or in bait containers.

THREATS: They form very dense, tangled mats in the upper portion of the water column, which subsequently shades out other aquatic plants below them, often to the point where the native species are nearly extirpated. The dense mats also can interfere with irrigation, hydroelectric plants, and recreational activities.

MANAGEMENT: Aquatic herbicides are effective in killing populations of watermilfoil. Mechanical methods such as weed harvesting, tilling, and dredging are often used. However, this may benefit the species because it can reproduce from stem fragments. Biocontrol through plant-pathogenic fungi has been used with some success. Public awareness campaigns are also used, typically by placing informative signs at boat launches, asking people to remove the aquatic plants from their boats when they leave.

Pastinaca sativa

WILD PARSNIP

DESCRIPTION: An herbaceous biennial (sometimes perennial), up to 6½ ft. (2 m) in height. Leaves are alternate, and once or twice pinnately compound. They can get up to 15¾ in. (40 cm) long, but progressively get smaller as you go up the stem. Flowers are borne in a flattened compound umbel, up to 8 in. (20 cm) across. Individual flowers are very small, with five yellow petals that curl under. It has a long taproot that is used as a root vegetable.

NATIVE DISTRIBUTION: It is native to a large part of Europe and western Asia.

NORTH AMERICAN DISTRIBUTION: It is widely distributed throughout most of North America, seemingly absent from only the boreal regions of Canada.

DATE(S) AND MEANS OF INTRODUCTION: The precise date and location of introduction are unknown, but it was likely one of the first plants brought to the New World in the 17th century. Its subsequent spread is thought to be primarily due to escaping from cultivation.

THREATS: It is able to reproduce prolifically, forming dense stands that can crowd out and displace native vegetation. The sap in stems and leaves contains a chemical that causes photodermatitis on humans and other animals that have exposed skin. It results in blisters and a burning sensation, somewhat similar to poison ivy.

MANAGEMENT: Mechanical controls such as mowing and cutting can be done, but the work should be timed so that it is performed prior to seed formation. Various herbicides are also effective in killing plants. Workers performing control activities should dress appropriately to prevent exposure to the sap.

Phalaris arundinacea

REED CANARY GRASS

DESCRIPTION: A perennial, rhizomatous species of grass, up to 6½ ft. (2 m) in height. Leaves are flat and smooth, up to 13¾ in. (35 cm) long and 1 in. (25 mm) wide. The inflorescence is a terminal panicle. It tends to grow in open habitats with moist soils, such as along lakeshores and in wet meadows.

NATIVE DISTRIBUTION: It is native to Eurasia and North America.

NORTH AMERICAN DISTRIBUTION: It is found throughout most of North America, including Alaska, Canada, Mexico, Puerto Rico, and most U.S. states outside of the southeastern part of the country.

DATE(S) AND MEANS OF INTRODUCTION: While it is considered native to North America, due to early records from the time period prior to widespread settlement and agriculture, the noxious plants found today are likely cultivars introduced from other countries and hybrids of the two.

THREATS: Once established, Reed Canary Grass vigorously spreads via rhizomes. It can form pure dense stands, inhibiting the growth of other species to the point where they are eliminated. From the time of establishment, it can take as little as 15 years for it to become the dominant species. It also has a low value to wildlife populations, as it is only used as a food source by a few species, and the stems grow too densely to provide a suitable habitat and cover.

MANAGEMENT: Managing Reed Canary Grass is challenging because it produces a segmented rhizome. All rhizome segments must be eradicated to prevent regrowth in treated areas. The most successful way of dealing with an infestation is through an integrated approach, using physical and chemical methods along with specific crop rotations that effectively control the weed. In large areas, a recommended strategy is to cut the grass in one season, apply herbicide the next, and burn in the following year.

Phellodendron amurense

AMUR CORK TREE

DESCRIPTION: Medium-size deciduous tree known for its uniquely textured corky bark. The Amur Cork Tree is a commonly planted ornamental in North America. Female trees produce green inflorescences that turn into persistent clusters of black berries, attractive to wildlife in the winter months.

NATIVE DISTRIBUTION: It is natively found from Japan to southern Russia, and—most notably—in a region called the Amur Oblast.

NORTH AMERICAN DISTRIBUTION: This tree is planted with surprising frequency amongst the Great Lakes states as an ornamental, despite indications of it invading disturbed areas with relative frequency.

DATE(S) AND MEANS OF INTRODUCTION: It was introduced into the United States as an ornamental shade tree in 1856.

THREATS: The persistent clusters of black berries are favored by wildlife in winter months, making them a vector of the spread. A single tree can produce thousands of berries, and seeds are viable in the soil for 1 to 2 years. Additionally, the species is allelopathic, releasing chemicals from its roots that alter the conditions of the soil to outcompete the plants around it. There is anecdotal evidence of a male variety of Amur Cork Tree producing fruit, but it is unknown how common this is without further study. Because of its adaptability, allelopathy, and how readily it reproduces, it is easily capable of displacing native understory species.

MANAGEMENT: It would be wise to cease planting Amur Cork Trees until more is known about the nature of the male individual's ability to produce female flowers. To control the spread of an already established tree, you could remove inflorescences before they become berries, and remove any sprouts that might survive in the area. This species vigorously stump-sprouts, making it especially important to apply the appropriate pesticides after removal.

Phyllostachys aureosulcata

YELLOW GROOVE BAMBOO

DESCRIPTION: A fast-growing bamboo with a dark-green stem with yellow streaks down the opposite sides of the culm. In older plants, the culm may become primarily yellow with green stripes.

NATIVE DISTRIBUTION: This species is native to the Zhejiang, Jiangsu, and Anhui provinces of China.

NORTH AMERICAN DISTRIBUTION: It is found throughout North America, with naturalized populations in the eastern and western coastal United States, and Canada.

DATE(S) AND MEANS OF INTRODUCTION: This species was first introduced into North America in 1908 from China for horticultural applications and landscaping.

THREATS: Yellow Groove Bamboo is uniquely cold hardy and poses a tremendous risk of becoming a ubiquitous invader with naturalized populations throughout North America. It can grow up to three feet per day and rapidly spreads via rhizomes. Dense monocultures of Yellow Groove Bamboo alter the habitat, severely limiting food sources for native species. The dense stands create perching sites for birds that defecate into the bamboo stands, creating a severe health risk for humans. The bird droppings harbor *Histoplasma capsulatum* spores, a fungus that is the causal agent of the respiratory disease histoplasmosis. This disease can cause pneumonia, extreme fatigue, body aches and pain, and—in about 8 percent of cases—death.

MANAGEMENT: The most effective prevention strategy is not using Yellow Groove Bamboo in the landscape. New infestations should be eradicated immediately, as removing well-established stands is challenging. Most control involves manually removing all plant material and digging into the ground to ensure all rhizomes are removed. Failure to remove rhizomes will ensure new growth will occur at treated locations. Chemical control of this species is not effective because the rhizomes are chambered. Any portion of a chambered rhizome that is not exposed to a chemical control agent will survive to produce a new population of Yellow Groove Bamboo.

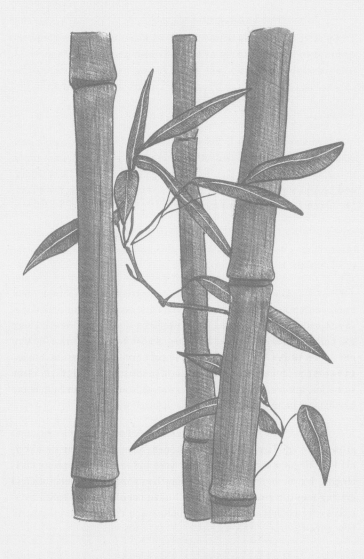

Pueraria montana

KUDZU

DESCRIPTION: A perennial semiwoody vine in the pea family that grows exceptionally fast, up to 12 in. (30 cm) per day. Mature stems are dark brown, woody, and up to 4 in. (10 cm) in diameter. Plants climb using tendrils; stems can root at the nodes, forming secondary root crowns. Up to 30 stems can be produced from one root crown.

NATIVE DISTRIBUTION: It is native to much of Southeast Asia.

NORTH AMERICAN DISTRIBUTION: It is now found in at least 30 U.S. states and one Canadian province (Ontario). It is most common in the southern states. Still, it has been reported as far north as Detroit and Boston and as far west as Texas and southeast Nebraska, with isolated occurrences in Hawaii and Oregon.

DATE(S) AND MEANS OF INTRODUCTION: Kudzu was widely planted in the South during the late 1800s and early 1900s, primarily for erosion control.

THREATS: Due to its rapid growth, ability to climb, and formation of massive, smothering mats, Kudzu has a significant impact on the diversity of native flora and fauna. It is estimated that Kudzu covers about 7.4 million acres (3 million hectares) across North America. Kudzu infestation causes both a significant impact on biodiversity and a massive economic impact through the loss of productive land areas. In many scenarios, it is less cost-effective to eradicate Kudzu and rehabilitate the land for production than to ignore the infestation.

MANAGEMENT: Controlling Kudzu is challenging due to its rapid growth rate and large underground storage tubers that sprout new populations. Regular mowing to remove vines and exhaust storage organs is an effective, multiyear control strategy. Using infested areas as animal grazing sites can also help to reduce Kudzu populations. Chemical control is effective but also requires a multiseason approach to exhaust all new growth.

Pyrus calleryana

BRADFORD PEAR, CALLERY PEAR

DESCRIPTION: The Bradford Pear is an attractive deciduous tree with a characteristic tear-shaped growth form. Branches and stems may produce sharp thorns. Leaves are alternately arranged and round to oval. Clusters of showy white flowers bloom in the early spring and have a strong, unpleasant odor. The fruit is small, brown, and almost woody in texture.

NATIVE DISTRIBUTION: Seeds used to breed the Bradford Pear were collected during an expedition to China in the early 20th century.

NORTH AMERICAN DISTRIBUTION: The Bradford Pear has been reported throughout North America, with the highest population density in the American Midwest, where it was most abundantly planted in landscapes.

DATE(S) AND MEANS OF INTRODUCTION: The Bradford Pear cultivar was selected as a disease-resistant rootstock in the early 20th century, collected from China by Frank Meyer, the same plant breeder who developed the famous Meyer lemon. Years later, this selection became a popular landscape tree and was planted throughout North America in the mid-1960s through the mid-2000s.

THREATS: The Bradford Pear can form dense thickets that outcompete native species. It produces leaves much earlier than native tree species, thereby shading out ephemeral understory species.

MANAGEMENT: A key aspect of Bradford Pear management is preventing the sale and use of these trees in the landscape. The Bradford Pear is still sold and regularly used in landscapes. Existing plantings should be cut down, and stumps treated with glyphosate or triclopyr. Larger trees can be girdled to prevent the production of more seed.

Rhamnus cathartica

BUCKTHORN

DESCRIPTION: Buckthorn is a medium-size deciduous tree. It has glossy green leaves on alternate branches. Copious quantities of inedible purple berries are produced in the fall.

NATIVE DISTRIBUTION: Buckthorn is native throughout Europe and parts of Asia.

NORTH AMERICAN DISTRIBUTION: It is broadly distributed in North America, with the highest populations of Buckthorn found in the American Midwest and northeastern states.

DATE(S) AND MEANS OF INTRODUCTION: It was initially brought to North America by European settlers in the late 18th century and primarily used as a landscape plant and hedge plant.

THREATS: Buckthorn outcompetes native species in forest habitats. It causes a loss of plant species biodiversity because less habitats are available for less competitive species. Its open structure makes nesting birds more vulnerable to predation.

MANAGEMENT: Prevention is accomplished through educational campaigns and by banning the distribution of plants and seeds. Eradication campaigns have been widely deployed, involving repeatedly removing trees and seedlings. The application of the herbicide 2,4-D on the surface of stumps improves efficacy.

Rosa multiflora

MULTIFLORA ROSE

DESCRIPTION: A large shrub with panicles of up to 30 showy, white flowers. It produces large orangish to red fruits.

NATIVE DISTRIBUTION: It is native to East Asia.

NORTH AMERICAN DISTRIBUTION: *Rosa multiflora* is found in the highest density across the eastern tier of the United States and adjacent areas of Canada along the West Coast.

DATE(S) AND MEANS OF INTRODUCTION: It was widely planted throughout the United States in the early 1900s and has become established and invasive throughout most of North America.

THREATS: It forms large, dense thickets that are difficult to move through for both people and animals. It degrades forage areas and makes it more difficult for foraging animals to access forageable food.

MANAGEMENT: *Rosa multiflora* is a challenging species to eradicate, due to its tough, spiny stems and deep roots from which new plants can emerge. Cutting down large stems and mowing every several weeks over a multiyear period is reported to be one of the most effective methods to eradicate *Rosa multiflora*. Applying the herbicide glyphosate or triclopyr to cut stems may speed up the process. A controversial biocontrol strategy has been developed that uses a mite to transmit a viral pathogen to the plants, but this strategy is condemned by the American Rose Society.

Salvinia molesta

GIANT SALVINIA, WATER FERN, KARIBA WEED

DESCRIPTION: Free-floating aquatic ferns, up to 12 in. (30 cm) long. Leaves are in whorls of three, one of which is submerged while the other two are floating. The leaf is round to elliptical in shape, up to $1^1/_5$ in. (3 cm) long and ¾ in. (2 cm) wide, and mostly hairy. Under favorable conditions, Giant Salvinia can form a thick, dense mat of vegetation.

NATIVE DISTRIBUTION: It is native to southeastern Brazil.

NORTH AMERICAN DISTRIBUTION: It can be found in Guatemala, Mexico, several Caribbean islands, and 23 U.S. states along the coasts and throughout the South.

DATE(S) AND MEANS OF INTRODUCTION: It appears to have first been reported in North America in the late 1970s. It likely arrived via the aquatic plant trade, as it is a popular aquatic plant for aquarium and water garden enthusiasts.

THREATS: Dense mats of this plant can shade out other aquatic vegetation, while also depleting the water of dissolved oxygen, having a broad ecological impact on the water bodies it is infesting. The thick mats also impede boat traffic, thus affecting recreational and commercial activities. The mats are known to harbor mosquitoes that transmit human disease. Giant Salvinia is also able to reproduce vegetatively from even small fragments of plant. Lastly, the mats can be thick enough to trick animals into walking on them, possibly causing them to drown, or otherwise become injured.

MANAGEMENT: Mechanical removal of the plants can be effective in controlling and eliminating this species, but only early on. The older and thicker the vegetative mat gets, the harder it is to effectively remove the plants mechanically. Herbicides can be used, but they must be used in conjunction with a surfactant (a substance that reduces water tension) because the hairs create a waterproof barrier that effectively shields the plant from herbicides. There has been success in using an aquatic weevil native to South America as a biological control agent. Inspection and quarantine of shipped goods are also used to prevent these plants from reaching non-native areas.

Securigera varia

CROWN VETCH

DESCRIPTION: A perennial legume that readily spreads via rhizomes. It is a low, spreading plant that has pinnately compound leaves up to 6¼ in. (16 cm) long, with 7 to 25 leaflets. Flowers are white to purple in color, with the typical legume (pea) shape.

NATIVE DISTRIBUTION: It is native to central Europe, with some also believing it to be native to parts of Asia and North Africa.

NORTH AMERICAN DISTRIBUTION: It is found in all U.S. states, most Canadian provinces, and isolated occurrences in Mexico.

DATE(S) AND MEANS OF INTRODUCTION: The earliest reference is from 1869, when it was reported along the Hudson River in New York. In the 1950s, it was widely planted in the United States as an ornamental cover crop and for erosion control. By the 1960s, it was established and abundant across much of the eastern United States.

THREATS: Because of its aggressive rates of growth and reproduction, it outcompetes native vegetation. This decreases biodiversity and alters other ecological processes.

MANAGEMENT: A combination of strategies is needed to eradicate an established colony successfully. These strategies include manually pulling plants, mowing, prescribed burns, and herbicide treatments. It is a regulated invasive species in many U.S. states, and there are widespread awareness campaigns to educate the public about the threats associated with this species.

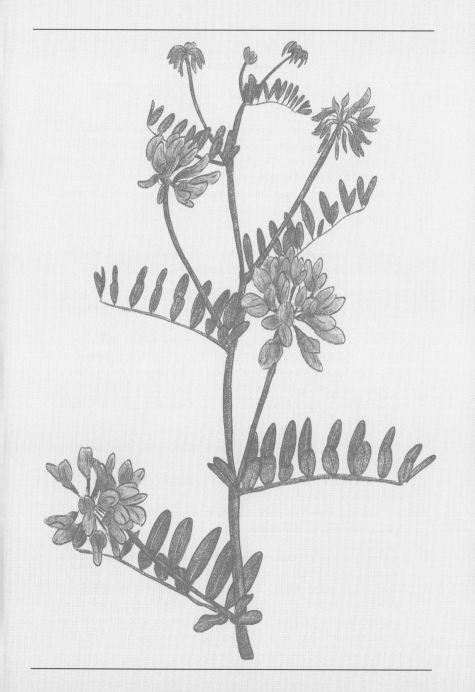

Sorghum halepense

JOHNSON GRASS

DESCRIPTION: A perennial grass that has an extensive, fleshy rhizome network. It can reach up to 10 ft. (3 m) in height on stems up to ¾ in. (2 cm) in diameter. The leaves are up to 23½ in. (60 cm) long and 1²/₅ in. (3.5 cm) wide. The flowers are borne in a many-branched panicle up to 19¾ in. (50 cm) long. The individual spikelets are ¹/₆ to ¼ in. (4 to 7 mm) long and oval.

NATIVE DISTRIBUTION: The exact native range of this species has not been fully resolved, but it most likely includes parts of southern Europe, the Mediterranean region, North Africa, and southern Asia.

NORTH AMERICAN DISTRIBUTION: It is currently found throughout most of North America, primarily absent from parts of the Great Plains and northern Rockies and areas north of those regions.

DATE(S) AND MEANS OF INTRODUCTION: It is believed to have been brought to the United States in the early 1800s and was a common forage crop by the 1830s. By the turn of the century, it was apparent that it was a problematic weed. It was first found in Canada (Ontario) in 1959.

THREATS: Johnson Grass has a vigorously spreading rhizome system and a high seed production rate. The vigorous spread makes it difficult to eradicate once established. It outcompetes native vegetation and other crops, reduces soil fertility, is a human allergen, can be toxic to livestock, and is a host to several plant pathogens. In severe infestations, it can reduce crop yield by 50 percent.

MANAGEMENT: Managing Johnson Grass is challenging because it produces a segmented rhizome. All rhizome segments must be eradicated to prevent regrowth in treated areas. The most successful way of dealing with an infestation is through an integrated approach, using physical and chemical methods along with specific crop rotations that effectively control the weed. Chemical control methods should be alternated between other modes of management.

Striga asiatica

WITCHWEED

DESCRIPTION: A hemiparasitic plant—one that gains energy through parasitism and photosynthesis. The aboveground plant does not present any sign that it is parasitic; rather, it looks like a typical plant, reaching heights of about 12 in. (30 cm). The leaves are narrow and lanceolate and appear opposite, and each successive pair of leaves is perpendicular to the leaves above and/or below it. Small, bilaterally symmetrical flowers are loosely borne in axillary spikes, and can be found in just about any color except blue. Underground, the stems are white, with scalelike leaves. The roots are succulent and are attached to the root system of the host plant. Symptoms of a heavy infestation include wilting, stunting, and scorched leaves.

NATIVE DISTRIBUTION: Witchweed is native to Africa and Asia.

NORTH AMERICAN DISTRIBUTION: In North America, it is currently only known to be in North and South Carolina.

DATE(S) AND MEANS OF INTRODUCTION: It was first identified in the Carolinas in 1955 but had likely been present for at least several years prior. It is thought that it was accidentally imported in fodder from Africa.

THREATS: It parasitizes many important cereal crops, including sorghum, corn, millet, rice, and sugarcane. Under normal moisture regimes, it is usually not a problem, but if the host plants are stressed, such as during a drought, the parasite can cause complete crop failure.

MANAGEMENT: Witchweed is a rare example of an invasive species management plan that has been effective. In North America, populations of Witchweed have decreased by 94 percent from peak population densities observed in the 1970s. Management plans have focused in part on the unique biology of Witchweed. For example, it grows best in dry conditions, and heavy irrigation in infested areas can reduce Witchweed populations.

Tamarix ramosissima

SALT CEDAR

DESCRIPTION: Salt Cedar is an attractive deciduous shrub that reaches about 13 ft. (4 m) tall and 10 ft. (3 m) wide. Branches are long and flowing, and leaves are feathery. It produces small but showy pink flowers clustered on long, terminal racemes.

NATIVE DISTRIBUTION: Salt Cedar is native to the Middle East.

NORTH AMERICAN DISTRIBUTION: In North America, Salt Cedar is primarily found in the Great Plains and areas west of that region.

DATE(S) AND MEANS OF INTRODUCTION: They were first reported in North America in 1837 in a New Jersey nursery. They were widely used in the western United States as ornamental plants and windbreaks, and to stabilize stream banks.

THREATS: Salt Cedar grows along the shoreline of a body of water in a region called the riparian zone. It produces a very long root system that grows below the water table to an area completely saturated with water called the phreatic zone. Plants like the Salt Cedar that use this water acquisition strategy are called phreatophytes, and there are some examples of these plants that have roots up to 98 ft. (30 m) deep! Salt Cedar is a very adaptable phreatophyte because it can survive in both freshwater and brackish water, and it has a very high reproductive rate and rapid growth rate. This means it can outcompete most native phreatophyte species, like willows, cottonwoods, and mulberry. More importantly, the excessive growth of Salt Cedar along the western river basins has caused significant groundwater depletion. It is estimated that about one-third of the water redirected from the Rio Grande is taken up by invasive Salt Cedars, causing hundreds of millions of dollars of loss.

MANAGEMENT: Salt Cedars invade degraded and disturbed land. An effective prevention strategy should include maintaining high-quality ecosystems with diverse populations of native species in the riparian zones that Salt Cedar infests. Once an infestation has occurred, management can be challenging. Mowing and burning is not an effective eradication strategy because the plants quickly grow back from basal stems. A combination strategy of cutting or mowing and applying the herbicide triclopyr to the stumps does reduce populations, but continual monitoring is required for maintenance.

Trapa natans

WATER CALTROP, WATER CHESTNUT

DESCRIPTION: An herbaceous annual aquatic plant, with flexible stems up to 16½ ft. (5 m) long. At the tip of the stem is a rosette of floating leaves, each with a broad triangular or deltoid shape, approximately 2 in. (5 cm) across and with serrated margins. The submerged stem has alternate leaves that are finely dissected and feather-like, up to 6 in. (15 cm) long. Flowers are small and white, with four petals, and emerge from the axils of the floating leaves. The fruit develops underwater and is about 1¹/₅ in. (3 cm) wide. It has a very distinctive appearance, which can best be described as "bat-like." The fruit also has four stout spines.

NATIVE DISTRIBUTION: It has a very broad but discontinuous native range across Asia, Africa, and Europe.

NORTH AMERICAN DISTRIBUTION: It is presently found in the northeastern part of North America, from New Hampshire to North Carolina and north to eastern Ontario and Quebec.

DATE(S) AND MEANS OF INTRODUCTION: It was first introduced into North America in the 1870s, in Massachusetts, where it was planted in a pond at the Arnold Arboretum of Harvard University and other nearby water bodies.

THREATS: It is able to form very dense mats of vegetation along the surface of the water, as many as 50 rosettes in one square meter. This shades out native aquatic vegetation and depletes dissolved oxygen concentrations, resulting in a loss of biodiversity. Water Caltrop is able to propagate vegetatively from pieces of stem or leaf, making mechanical control an ineffective method of eradication. Additionally, the seeds can remain viable for 10 years. The dense floating mats can also impede boat traffic, and the spines on the fruit can cause injury to swimmers. A species of fluke that can infect humans spends part of its life cycle on this plant, and consuming the fish uncooked could result in an intestinal fluke infection.

MANAGEMENT: Control and eradication are more likely to be successful if an infestation is caught early on. Therefore, awareness campaigns have been created to inform the public about the dangers the plant poses, as well as to give instructions on reporting populations of it. An additional way to curb the spread is the cleaning of boating and other recreational equipment upon leaving a water body. Many states have legislation that regulates commerce of this species. Manual removal can be somewhat effective in small infestations, although care must be taken to avoid releasing fragments of vegetation that can then turn into new plants. The chemical application of herbicides is often used in conjunction with manual removal, although even this combination is not 100 percent effective.

Triadica sebifera

CHINESE TALLOW TREE

DESCRIPTION: A species of tree in the spurge family, reaching heights of 50 ft. (15 m). Leaves are alternate, with a rhomboid (rhombus-like) to ovate shape and an acuminate (tapered) tip. The leaves can grow up to 5 in. (13 cm) long and 3½ in. (9 cm) wide. Yellowish-green flowers are borne in terminal racemes up to 13¾ in. (35 cm) long that are usually hanging downward. Individual flowers are small and three parted.

NATIVE DISTRIBUTION: It is native to China.

NORTH AMERICAN DISTRIBUTION: It is found primarily in the southeastern United States, from Virginia to Arkansas and points south. There are also occurrences in Mexico and California.

DATE(S) AND MEANS OF INTRODUCTION: The Chinese Tallow Tree was brought to the United States in 1772 by Benjamin Franklin, with the intent to use it as a source of oil and wax. In the early 1900s, it was widely planted for both commercial and ornamental reasons.

THREATS: It is a fast-growing, vigorously spreading tree that can form pure, dense stands that displace and kill off native plant species, resulting in a cascading effect on biodiversity and ecosystem processes. Many native coastal grasslands and prairies of the southeastern United States are now thickets of this tree.

MANAGEMENT: A combination of mechanical and chemical control is the most effective solution for eradication. This involves hand removal of younger plants, or cutting of larger plants, followed by chemical treatment of the cut stumps. The Chinese Tallow Tree species readily grows suckers (small shoots at the base of the tree), so simply cutting the trees down just initiates the formation of suckers.

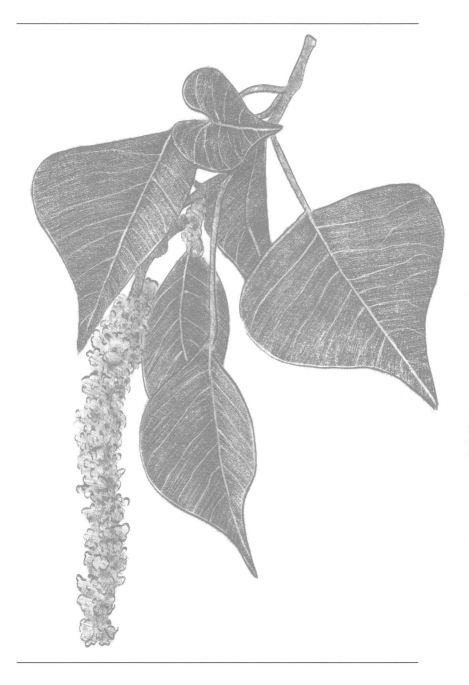

Tribulus terrestris

GOATHEAD, PUNCTURE VINE

DESCRIPTION: A prostrate annual or perennial herb in the caltrop family. The hairy stems are branched and can reach up to 6½ ft. (2 m) long. Leaves are opposite and pinnately compound, up to 2¾ in. (7 cm) long. Individual leaves have three to eight pairs of lanceolate leaflets that are up to ³/₅ in. (15 mm) long and ¹/₅ in. (5 mm) wide. In each pair of opposite leaves, one is usually noticeably larger than the other. Solitary flowers are borne in the axils of the smaller leaf of the pair of opposite leaves. The yellow flowers have five petals, with the flower being about ³/₅ in. (15 mm) in diameter. The fruit is a woody burr about ²/₅ in. (1 cm) wide. When ripe, it splits into four to five segments, each of which bears two spines and contains one to four yellow seeds.

NATIVE DISTRIBUTION: It is native to the Mediterranean region.

NORTH AMERICAN DISTRIBUTION: Goathead can be found from Central America to the northern United States, absent only in the northern Great Lakes, northern Great Plains, and northern New England.

DATE(S) AND MEANS OF INTRODUCTION: The exact dates of introduction into North America are not known, but records of it exist back to at least the 1940s. It is thought that it was spread worldwide as seeds stuck to the wool of sheep or in hay or manure.

THREATS: It can outcompete many crop species due to its long tap-root, which allows it to survive drought conditions. The spiny fruits are designed to stick to animal fur, which facilitates further spread from areas where it becomes established. The spines are also stout enough that they can cause injuries when consumed or stepped on by both humans and livestock. Seeds can remain viable in the soil for many years, and they can germinate at any time of the year, leading to recurrences in areas it was thought to have been eradicated. The plant is also toxic to sheep, goats, and cattle and is especially problematic during droughts, when little other vegetation is available for animals to eat. A three-year drought during the 1980s in Australia killed upward of 20,000 sheep via consumption of this plant. Lastly, it is an alternate host for several plant pathogens.

MANAGEMENT: Because of the seed viability, and the fact that they can flower and set seed rather quickly, control of this species requires especially vigilant monitoring and action to prevent Goathead plants from going to seed. Shallow plowing and mechanical burr removal are techniques often used to keep seeds from getting released. Soil solarization is another technique that is effective. This involves the application of clear plastic sheets or mulch, which acts as a greenhouse, heating the soil to a temperature that the plant cannot withstand. Most herbicides are effective in controlling this species and are commonly employed. There has been some success using imported weevils that feed on it.

Vincetoxicum nigrum

BLACK SWALLOWWORT

DESCRIPTION: An herbaceous perennial species of vine that is in the same family as milkweed (Apocynaceae). It has twining pubescent stems that reach up to 10 ft. (3 m) in length. Along the stem are pairs of opposite leaves up to 4¾ in. (12 cm) long that are ovate in shape, with a pointed tip. Flowers are borne in cymes from the leaf axils, usually bearing 6 to 10 flowers per cyme. Flowers are ¼ to ⅓ in. (6 to 8 mm) in diameter, have five petals, and have a dark maroon to purple color. Like milkweeds, the seeds have a tuft of hairs to facilitate wind dispersal.

NATIVE DISTRIBUTION: It is native to Portugal, Spain, France, and Italy.

NORTH AMERICAN DISTRIBUTION: Black Swallowwort is mostly found in the region of Nova Scotia to Minnesota, south to Kentucky, and in Maryland. There are sporadic and isolated occurrences farther west.

DATE(S) AND MEANS OF INTRODUCTION: It was first observed in 1854 in Massachusetts. It is most likely a garden escapee in the areas it has been found.

THREATS: Black Swallowwort can form dense, tangled masses that effectively shade out and eliminate other plant species, resulting in a loss of biodiversity. Because it is related to milkweed, monarch butterflies will lay eggs on this species; however, it appears that most caterpillars from these eggs die early on. Thus, this species could have a detrimental impact on monarch butterfly populations.

MANAGEMENT: The best tactic to control this species is early detection and eradication. They are susceptible to certain herbicides, which is one means of eradicating the species. Mechanical and biological control methods, so far, have not been proven effective.

MICROORGANISMS

BACTERIA

Liberibacter spp. and *Diaphorina citri*

CITRUS GREENING DISEASE, YELLOW DRAGON DISEASE, HUANGLONGBING DISEASE (HLB)

DESCRIPTION: *Liberibacter* spp. are a unique group of bacteria that are restricted to the sieve tube cells of phloem in plants. These pathogens are vectored and transmitted by the Asian citrus psyllid, a small plant-eating insect. When the psyllid feeds on an infected plant, it harbors the *Liberibacter* bacterium in its mouthparts and transmits the pathogen to a new host when it feeds again.

NATIVE DISTRIBUTION: It is native to southwestern Asia.

NORTH AMERICAN DISTRIBUTION: The disease has been reported in Florida, Mexico, and, most recently, California.

DATE(S) AND MEANS OF INTRODUCTION: The disease was first observed in Florida in 1998, with the inoculum source undetermined.

THREATS: Citrus Greening Disease causes citrus fruits to become deformed, hard, and inedible. Infected trees eventually die. There is no cure or treatment. To date, Citrus Greening Disease has caused losses of over $4 billion in revenue in Florida alone.

MANAGEMENT: There is no treatment for Citrus Greening Disease. The disease is prevented by eliminating the insect vector, vigilant scouting for new disease, and immediate removal of any trees that are suspected to be infected. Good sanitation practices include the incineration of diseased plant material and strict adherence to quarantine procedures.

Ralstonia solanacearum

SOUTHERN BACTERIAL WILT

DESCRIPTION: A species of pathogenic bacteria that causes Southern Bacterial Wilt on a wide variety of plants (more than 250 species). Symptoms can be variable, depending on the bacterial strain and the infected species, but typically begin with drooping or wilting leaves during the day, followed by recovery at night. This is usually followed by a noticeable discoloration (mostly brownish) on the stems. Eventually, the wilting fails to recover at night, leading to the death of the plant. An oozing substance may come out of any part of the plant that is wounded or cut.

NATIVE DISTRIBUTION: It is difficult to pinpoint where this bacteria originated. There are several strains, one of which is considered native to the southeastern United States. It is considered endemic wherever it is found.

NORTH AMERICAN DISTRIBUTION: It is found throughout almost the entirety of North America.

DATE(S) AND MEANS OF INTRODUCTION: Southern Bacterial Wilt was first reported in the South in the late 1800s on tomato plants. It is unknown if this was a native strain or an introduced one. It has been shown to be transported on various host plant species internationally.

THREATS: It is a serious pest of many cultivated plants, including potato, tomato, tobacco, ginger, soybean, and banana. Yield reductions of up to 15 percent have been reported during outbreaks. It is readily transported around the world; it can survive for long periods of time on inorganic substrates and can be transmitted vertically (mother plant to seed).

MANAGEMENT: This is a difficult species to control. It is resistant to many antibiotics that are traditionally used in agriculture. The most effective way to control it is through the implementation of a crop management plan that utilizes strategies and techniques that negatively impact the bacteria. This includes things such as only planting seeds or tubers that are certified disease free, vigilance regarding the detection and reporting of disease occurrence, weed and pest management, irrigation management, and public education campaigns.

Xanthomonas citri ssp. *citri*

CITRUS CANKER

DESCRIPTION: A pathogenic bacteria that causes Citrus Canker in various types of citrus trees. Symptoms typically involve the appearance of lesions on leaves, twigs, and fruit, causing stunted growth, leaf fall, and premature fruit fall. It prefers areas with warm, humid climates and tends to only infect young trees and seedlings.

NATIVE DISTRIBUTION: It is believed to be native to China, Japan, and Hong Kong.

NORTH AMERICAN DISTRIBUTION: In North America, it is found primarily in areas in which citrus trees are grown. In the United States, it is known in Alabama, Florida, Louisiana, and Texas. Elsewhere, it is known to be present in the British Virgin Islands, Martinique, and Mexico.

DATE(S) AND MEANS OF INTRODUCTION: Citrus Canker was first found in the United States in 1910, near the Florida-Georgia border. It spreads via the transportation of infected fruit and seedlings.

THREATS: Outbreaks can have significant impacts on the fruit yield in affected orchards. Besides affecting the fruit, causing them to fall before ripening and/or having unsightly lesions on the skin, it retards the growth of younger trees, primarily through defoliation.

MANAGEMENT: A quarantine and inspection process is in place for the movement of oranges from regions the pathogen is endemic to, in order to prevent new infections. Management is challenging because no chemical or biological controls have been developed for large and well-established infections. The only management option is the removal of infected trees.

FUNGI

Bretziella fagacearum

OAK WILT

DESCRIPTION: Fungal pathogen affecting all species of oak. Red oak species are especially susceptible, experiencing a much more aggressive onset of symptoms and speed of decline than white oak species. Oak Wilt infection restricts the tree's vascular system, resulting in dieback in the crown. Leaves wilt back from the outer edges inward. Additionally, the pathogen produces fungal mats underneath the bark which eventually create fissures, enabling the introduction of more pests and pathogens.

NATIVE DISTRIBUTION: The true endemic range is unknown, but it is thought to have originated from somewhere in Central or South America.

NORTH AMERICAN DISTRIBUTION: This pathogen has been identified as far west as South Dakota to Texas, and as far east as New York to South Carolina. The Great Lakes states are considered hot spots for this pathogen, due to the climatic conditions from spring through summer.

DATE(S) AND MEANS OF INTRODUCTION: It was originally identified in Wisconsin in 1944, though the exact date and means of its introduction are unknown.

THREATS: Oak Wilt significantly threatens *Quercus* populations in areas it has been identified, causing rapid mortality. The disease is spread by beetles attracted to fungal mats, infected firewood, or root grafts.

MANAGEMENT: To reduce the spread of Oak Wilt, no pruning should be done from mid-April to mid-July, and other forms of damage should be prevented if possible. If the pathogen occurs in a pocket amongst healthy trees, the infected trees should be removed, and the wood burned as quickly as possible. Additionally, roots should be severed around infected trees to prevent root graft transmission. There are some pesticides available that help control the infection and spread as well.

Batrachochytrium dendrobatidis (Bd)

CHYTRIDIOMYCOSIS

DESCRIPTION: A fungal-like organism that can infect the skin of more than 350 species of amphibians. It ultimately causes the development of thick or necrotic skin, interfering with the salt-and-water balance in an amphibian's body, causing lethargy and ultimately death.

NATIVE DISTRIBUTION: While not confirmed, it is believed to have originated in Africa or possibly China. It currently has a global distribution.

NORTH AMERICAN DISTRIBUTION: It has been detected throughout much of North America.

DATE(S) AND MEANS OF INTRODUCTION: Chytridiomycosis was first discovered in 1998, and it was quickly realized that it had a global distribution. It most likely spread via the international trade of frogs for pet and aquarium purposes.

THREATS: An outbreak of this fungus has significant ecological impacts, with a marked decrease in amphibian population and biodiversity. This fungus has been directly associated with the decline of at least 28 critically endangered amphibian species. This has a domino effect on other components of local food webs and ecosystems. The fungus is highly adaptable and tolerant of a wide range of temperatures and moisture levels.

MANAGEMENT: No effective management strategies are developed, and scientific research in this area is not well funded. A better understanding of the biology and ecology of *Bd* is required to develop appropriate regulating policies and management practices to save amphibious species affected by this pathogen.

Cronartium ribicola

WHITE PINE BLISTER RUST

DESCRIPTION: A rust fungus that infects many species of white pine (*Pinus*) and currant (*Ribes*) and causes the disease White Pine Blister Rust. Symptoms include browning of all needles on a particular branch and sap-oozing cankers surrounded by pale orange blisters.

NATIVE DISTRIBUTION: White Pine Blister Rust is native to China.

NORTH AMERICAN DISTRIBUTION: It is found throughout Canada and the United States, wherever its host species (five-needle pine) is found.

DATE(S) AND MEANS OF INTRODUCTION: It was accidentally introduced into the United States in 1910. The further spread was likely due to natural and man-made processes.

THREATS: Infestations of this rust result in substantial long-term damage, if not death, of the host tree. Coupled with the fast rate of spread, entire stands of pine can be killed off by this fungus in a relatively short time. The disease has significant ecological impacts, endangering the stability or survival of white pine habitats and ecosystems. Susceptible *Ribes* species have reduced fruit yields when infected.

MANAGEMENT: Chemical control in forests is not very effective, primarily due to the logistics of treating isolated forests in rugged terrain. Fungicide application to pine seedlings in a nursery situation has proved effective. Eradication of *Ribes* in areas near pines has had some success. Several resistance-related genes have been found in various pine species, and breeding programs are underway in attempts to breed varieties that are resistant to the fungus.

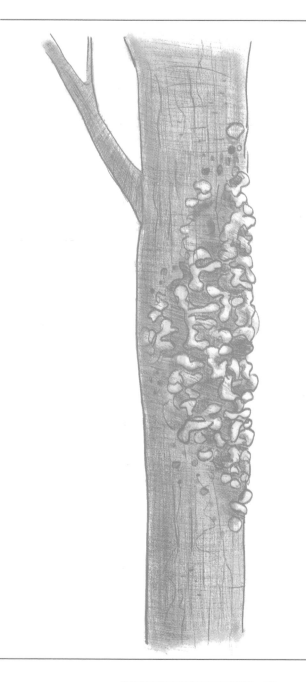

Cryphonectria parasitica

CHESTNUT BLIGHT

DESCRIPTION: A species of fungus that infects chestnut (*Castanea*) trees, causing the disease Chestnut Blight. Symptoms of Chestnut Blight are the appearance of small, flat, orange-brown lesions on smooth bark. These eventually develop into cankers, as well as the formation of tiny, yellowish stromata (spore-bearing fungal tissue) that burst through the bark. The canker ultimately girdles the tree, killing off the portion of the stem that is above it.

NATIVE DISTRIBUTION: It is native to China and Japan.

NORTH AMERICAN DISTRIBUTION: It is widespread throughout much of the United States, especially the eastern half, where the American chestnut (*Castanea dentata*) once was a dominant tree. It has also been detected in British Columbia and Ontario, Canada.

DATE(S) AND MEANS OF INTRODUCTION: It was first brought to North America, inadvertently, in 1904, when infected Japanese chestnuts (*Castanea crenata*) were imported for commercial purposes. The disease spreads via spores that enter wounds on the tree, such as when a branch breaks off.

THREATS: This fungus had a devastating impact on the native American chestnut, formerly one of the dominant trees in the eastern hardwood forests, providing food and habitats for a large number and variety of organisms. The blight does not outright kill the tree, but it does kill off stems before they are able to produce flowers and fruit, making the American chestnut functionally extinct. There are still isolated occurrences of mature American chestnuts around the country, either due to some innate resistance to the fungus or because they are isolated enough that they have not been exposed.

MANAGEMENT: In North America, no management practices are employed, because the American chestnut is considered largely extirpated.

Ophiostoma novo-ulmi

DUTCH ELM DISEASE

DESCRIPTION: A fungal pathogen of woody plants that causes Dutch Elm Disease. Symptoms of an infection include the wilting, yellowing, and dying of leaves, typically starting at the branch tip and gradually working its way toward the stem. Once the fungus reaches the main trunk, the tree will die within a year or two.

NATIVE DISTRIBUTION: The origin of the fungus is not known. One hypothesis is that it originated in eastern Asia, because the native elm species there are highly resistant to the fungus, indicating they have been coexisting for a very long time.

NORTH AMERICAN DISTRIBUTION: It can be found across seven Canadian provinces and 16 U.S. states.

DATE(S) AND MEANS OF INTRODUCTION: It is believed that the fungus emerged in the southern Great Lakes region during the 1940s, reaching both coasts by the early 1980s. This outbreak was preceded by an earlier outbreak of Dutch Elm Disease which was caused by a different but closely related species (*Ophiostoma ulmi*). The fungus is believed to have been introduced into North America via imports of timber.

THREATS: This fungus has had a devastating impact on elm populations worldwide. This obviously has a significant effect on those species that depend on elms for survival. Further, the loss of wild elms results in a change in the species composition of the forests they were found in, leading to a net loss of biodiversity.

MANAGEMENT: New infections are prevented by requiring a phytosanitary certificate for the transport of all elm trees and elm wood. Good sanitation practices, involving incinerating all infected wood and removing and burning all infected trees, can help reduce new disease incidence by up to 80 percent. Controlling the vectoring bark beetles (*Scolytus* and *Hylurgopinus*) is one facet of good sanitation. A biocontrol strategy using an engineered hypovirulent *Verticillium* fungus is commercially available. An integrated pest management (IPM) strategy employing the best practices of good sanitation, biocontrol, and chemical treatment may be either preventative or prophylactic and is recommended.

Phytophthora infestans

LATE BLIGHT

DESCRIPTION: A type of protist called an oomycete (water mold). They superficially resemble fungi with white mycelia but are more closely related to diatoms and brown algae.

NATIVE DISTRIBUTION: This pathogen likely originated in the Toluca Valley of Mexico. For nearly a century, it was believed to have evolved in South America.

NORTH AMERICAN DISTRIBUTION: It is found throughout North America, with cyclical periods of higher disease incidence.

DATE(S) AND MEANS OF INTRODUCTION: There has been considerable speculation about the origins of *Phytophthora infestans*, the causal agent of Late Blight of potatoes and tomatoes, and specifically speculation about the origin of the strain that caused the Irish Potato Famine. The most devastating disease and associated crop loss occurred in the 1840s, with smaller outbreaks in 1879 and the early 20th century. The original strain likely evolved in Mexico and arrived in the eastern United States in the early 1840s. The eastern states experienced significant crop loss due to Late Blight in the early 1940s, but the diversity of the potato cultivars grown there helped to prevent the devastating crop losses experienced by farmers in Ireland.

THREATS: Late Blight can cause total crop loss of potatoes and tomatoes under the right growing conditions—specifically cool, wet, and limited sunshine.

MANAGEMENT: The disease is prevented by following good sanitation practices, using certified disease-free stock, and growing resistant cultivars. The continued development of resistant and tolerant cultivars is an ongoing challenge for plant breeders.

Phytophthora ramorum

SUDDEN OAK DEATH

DESCRIPTION: A type of protist called an oomycete (water mold). They superficially resemble fungi with white mycelia but are more closely related to diatoms and brown algae.

NATIVE DISTRIBUTION: It is native to Japan.

NORTH AMERICAN DISTRIBUTION: In North America, it can be found in British Columbia, Canada, and at least 13 U.S. states. Occurrences are minimal and scattered in most of these states, except California, Oregon, and Washington.

DATE(S) AND MEANS OF INTRODUCTION: It was first identified in California in 2001. It can spread rapidly in the horticultural trade. Localized spreading is mostly through spores in wind and rain.

THREATS: It can infect many species, although the severity differs. It appears to be especially lethal to oaks (*Quercus*) and tanoaks (*Notholithocarpus*). It has killed over 50 million trees in the Pacific Northwest, radically changing the composition of the forests there. In addition, infected areas end up with many dead branches and other woody debris from the dying trees, significantly increasing the fire risk in these stands.

MANAGEMENT: Many strategies are employed (often simultaneously) to prevent new infections. A key challenge of prevention is detection, as diagnosing a *P. ramorum* infection by visual observation alone is difficult because the symptoms mirror those caused by other pathogens. Phosphites (molecules each comprised of a phosphorus atom and three oxygen atoms) can be injected into oak trees, usually offering about two years of protection. Resistant varieties of susceptible tree species have been bred, and planting nonsusceptible species among susceptible species also must limit the spread. Good sanitation of forestry tools and equipment before their use in a new area is a best practice to avoid new infections through wounds.

Pseudogymnoascus destructans

WHITE-NOSE SYNDROME

DESCRIPTION: A species of fungus that is adapted to cold temperatures and can infect bats during hibernation, causing a disease called White-Nose Syndrome. A fungal infection is apparent by the appearance of fungal growth on the wings and nose of a bat. When it has successfully infected a bat, the fungus causes a wide range of detrimental physiologic effects that can result in the bat's death.

NATIVE DISTRIBUTION: Its native range is currently unknown, with some evidence pointing to Europe.

NORTH AMERICAN DISTRIBUTION: It is currently known to be present in at least 33 U.S. states and five Canadian provinces, primarily in the eastern half of the continent.

DATE(S) AND MEANS OF INTRODUCTION: At this time, it is unknown how the fungus first arrived in North America. It was first discovered in New York in 2006 and has since spread quickly, primarily via physical contact between bats.

THREATS: The fungus can infect bats in all life stages and has a high mortality rate. It is believed to have already killed millions of bats in North America. Bats are a significant natural insect pest control, saving U.S. farmers $3 billion annually. This value certainly will decline as the population of bats is diminished.

MANAGEMENT: There is no effective method of preventing fungal spread or treatment for infected bats. The fungal spores have been found in the soil of bat resting sites and on the clothing of spelunkers exploring the caves. In 2012, a national protocol was developed for spelunkers and other cave enthusiasts, detailing best practices for preventing the spread of fungal spores to new locations. It recommends treating clothing and gear with hot water, as the fungus perishes above 68°F (20°C). Cave access is becoming more and more restricted, to prevent the spread of the fungus. Treatment with probiotic bacteria has shown promise in reducing the mortality rate of the infection.

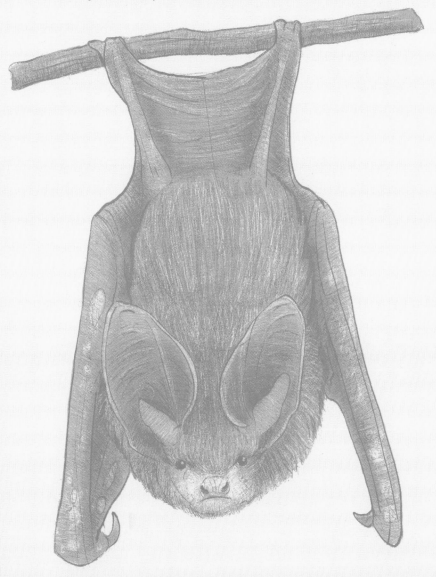

Puccinia graminis

WHEAT STEM RUST

DESCRIPTION: A species of rust fungus that infects both wild and cultivated species of grass, with over 400 identified host species. It has a complex, multistage life cycle, including one stage on an alternate host (*Berberis* spp.). Symptoms include the appearance of rust-colored spots or lesions on the host plant.

NATIVE DISTRIBUTION: It is considered to be native to western Asia; however, it is described in texts dating back at least 300 years in France, and 3,300-year-old wheat found in Israel had spores on it.

NORTH AMERICAN DISTRIBUTION: It is found throughout almost all of North America.

DATE(S) AND MEANS OF INTRODUCTION: It is not known exactly when Wheat Stem Rust reached North America, or how, but there was an outbreak in the United States in 1878. Spores are known to persist on plants and soil that are transported internationally, which is a likely cause of the current near-worldwide spread. Spores are also transported via the wind over very long distances.

THREATS: Outbreaks can cause significant mortality of cultivated grains and have been known to completely kill off a field over a couple of weeks. Historically, this had devastating economic impacts; however, the development of resistant cultivars has shifted the economic impact to the breeding and evaluation of resistant crops. That being said, there is at least one strain of Wheat Stem Rust, known as Ug99, that can infect over 90 percent of wheat grown worldwide. For this reason, this pathogen poses a significant threat to global food security.

MANAGEMENT: The primary management strategy for Wheat Stem Rust is the development and use of resistant cultivars. This, combined with chemical control and improved detection tools, is used to help manage the disease and monitor the likelihood of disease spread.

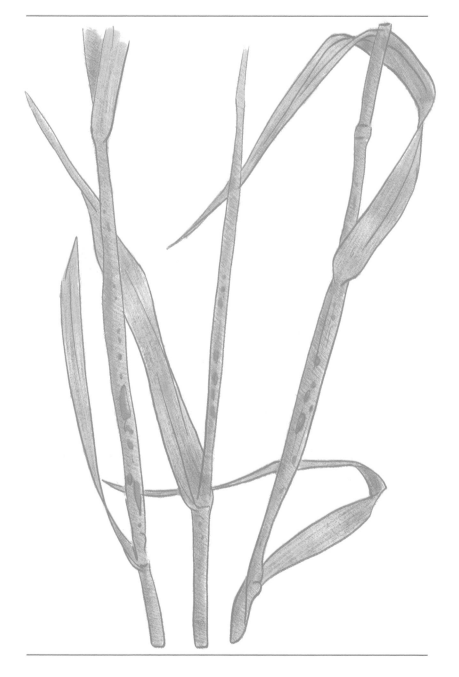

Raffaelea lauricola

LAUREL WILT

DESCRIPTION: *Raffaelea* is a fungus with white mycelia and brown spores. It is a fungal symbiont of the redbay ambrosia beetle (*Xyleborus glabratus*). *Raffaelea* infection causes the death of plants found in the laurel family.

NATIVE DISTRIBUTION: The redbay ambrosia beetle and its fungal symbiont, *Raffaelea lauricola*, are native to Japan, Taiwan, China, India, and Myanmar.

NORTH AMERICAN DISTRIBUTION: It is currently reported from the coastal areas of the southeastern United States.

DATE(S) AND MEANS OF INTRODUCTION: The redbay ambrosia beetle that vectors and transmits the disease was first reported in 2002 in Georgia. Laurel Wilt was first reported in 2004 in South Carolina.

THREATS: This pathogen can rapidly kill most woody plants in the laurel family, including avocado, bay laurel, cinnamon, and sassafras, to list just a few. Over the last nearly two decades, hundreds of millions of trees have been killed by this pathogen.

MANAGEMENT: No effective management strategies have been implemented, and only limited regulations on moving wood between infected and noninfected locations are in place. Effective management will require immediate restrictions on wood imports, which was likely the original method of introduction, and restrictions on the transport of wood from infected locations to other areas. New sources of disease resistance in laurel species are being researched.

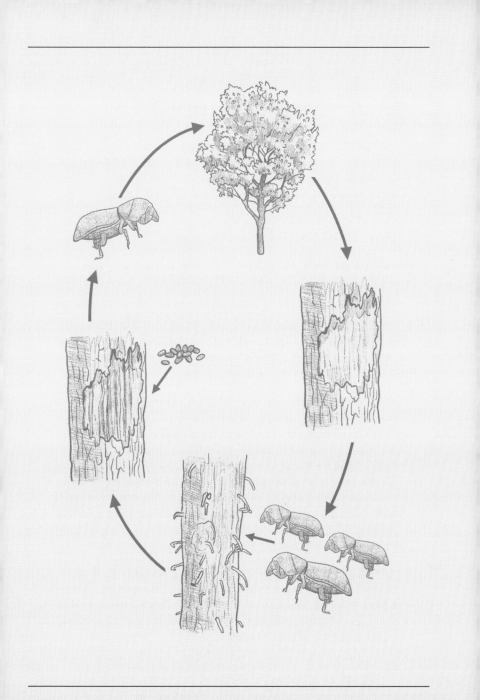

Tilletia indica

KARNAL BUNT

DESCRIPTION: A pathogenic fungus that causes Karnal Bunt of wheat. The fungi infect the developing seeds of wheat, partially destroying them and causing them to lose viability and fall. Symptoms are primarily the appearance of darkened seeds.

NATIVE DISTRIBUTION: It first emerged in Pakistan in 1909 and is believed to be endemic to that part of the world.

NORTH AMERICAN DISTRIBUTION: It is currently known to be present in Mexico and Arizona. It has been eradicated from four other states.

DATE(S) AND MEANS OF INTRODUCTION: It was first reported in Mexico in 1972 and in the southwestern United States in 1996. It likely arrived in North America via infected imported grain. Localized spreading is via windborne spores.

THREATS: The actual damage this disease causes to crops is minor, with the significant crop impact being on the quality of the seed. The fungus is difficult to detect and eradicate. It usually only infects a few seeds, thus making it difficult to identify in the field. It imparts a fishy taste to the harvested seeds, due to certain chemicals that are produced during infection. The most significant impact of Karnal Bunt is the economic costs associated with the import and export of the wheat crop. As one of the biggest exporters of wheat in the world, the United States is severely impacted by the quarantine measures and regulations surrounding the export of wheat infected with the fungus that causes Karnal Bunt.

MANAGEMENT: Management is challenging because no consistently effective chemical control strategies have been developed. Much work is focused on developing resistant or tolerant wheat varieties. A major component of disease management is prevention through the restricted import and export of infected wheat.

VIRUSES

Aphthovirus

HAND, FOOT, AND MOUTH DISEASE (HFMD)

DESCRIPTION: These are viruses that cause Hand, Foot, and Mouth Disease in cloven-hoofed animals. Symptoms of infection include fever and the appearance of a rash or blisters on the hands, feet, mouth, and/or buttocks. The disease is rarely fatal but can stunt growth and decrease milk production in livestock, and has been known to cause myocarditis.

NATIVE DISTRIBUTION: The exact time and place of the origin of this virus remain unknown.

NORTH AMERICAN DISTRIBUTION: At present, there are no known occurrences in North America, and the last outbreak was in the 1920s.

DATE(S) AND MEANS OF INTRODUCTION: It was first identified in the northeastern United States in 1870 and in Mexico in 1947. The means of introduction are not known.

THREATS: It is highly contagious, quickly spreading through close contact with an infected individual. During an outbreak, significant impacts on livestock growth and milk production can occur, even in recovered individuals. The best way to prevent further spread is the culling of infected animals, and if many animals are infected, many animals are killed, resulting in a significant economic impact.

MANAGEMENT: This virus is primarily controlled through the use of vaccines, which have proven to be quite effective.

MIDDLE EAST RESPIRATORY SYNDROME (MERS), MERS-COV

DESCRIPTION: MERS is a type of coronavirus in the same group as the COVID-19 virus. The zoonotic source of MERS is unknown. Typically rats and bats serve as reservoirs of the coronavirus; however, the MERS virus has been isolated from camels in the Middle East.

NATIVE DISTRIBUTION: It was first discovered in the Arabian Peninsula in 2012.

NORTH AMERICAN DISTRIBUTION: Although two cases of MERS-CoV have been reported in North America, there was no known spread of MERS. Transmission occurs from exposure to respiratory secretions, but the exact transmission pathway is poorly understood.

DATE(S) AND MEANS OF INTRODUCTION: Two cases of MERS-CoV have been reported in North America. Both cases were found in health-care workers who had recently traveled to Saudi Arabia or had direct, extended contact with an infected individual.

THREATS: The MERS virus causes a severe respiratory infection, resulting in death in about 37 percent of those infected. The fatality rate may be artificially inflated because individuals with a mild illness may not be aware of their infection status to know to report it. To date, 2,500 cases have been reported worldwide, resulting in approximately 800 deaths. Although the risk of exposure is currently very low in North America, the MERS virus poses a serious threat to human health and safety. Individuals who travel to the Middle East, interact with dromedary camels, or care for infected individuals are at the highest risk of contracting MERS.

MANAGEMENT: To prevent a U.S. epidemic, the Centers for Disease

Control and Prevention (CDC) monitors the global status of MERS closely. To date, over 1,300 individuals in North America have been tested for suspected or potential MERS, but as mentioned earlier, only two cases have been discovered. There is no standardized treatment for infection; individuals with severe cases are treated for symptoms.

Ebolavirus

EBOLA, EBOLA HEMORRHAGIC FEVER, EBOLA VIRUS DISEASE (EVD)

DESCRIPTION: Four different viruses in the genus *Ebolavirus* cause EVD in humans. *Ebolavirus* is a single-stranded RNA virus, with virions shaped like a shepherd's crook, a 6, or a U.

NATIVE DISTRIBUTION: *Ebolavirus* is endemic to the tropical regions of Africa.

NORTH AMERICAN DISTRIBUTION: Only 11 cases of EVD are known to have occurred in North America.

DATE(S) AND MEANS OF INTRODUCTION: Between 2014 and 2016, nine health-care workers were evacuated to the United States for treatment during the West African EVD epidemic. Subsequently, two new cases occurred in health-care workers who contracted EVD from treating the initially infected individuals.

THREATS: *Ebolavirus* infection is rare and currently not found in North America. Although EVD outbreaks only rarely occur, they have severe consequences for humans. The disease causes Ebola Hemorrhagic Fever. More specifically, *Ebolavirus* infection causes disseminated intra-vascular coagulation (DIC), a condition that causes blood clots to form in small blood vessels throughout the body. This clogs those vessels, and it uses up the clotting factors needed in the rest of the blood supply. This can lead to uncontrolled bleeding from many sites on the body. Infection is deadly in 25 to 90 percent of cases. The West African Ebola Pandemic of 2014 to 2016 infected over 28,000 individuals and resulted in over 11,000 deaths.

MANAGEMENT: Prevention is the most essential aspect of managing *Ebolavirus*. Public education campaigns emphasize the importance of proper preparation and handling of wild meat to prevent wildlife-to-human transmission. They also inform the public about best practices to avoid human-to-human transmission. As the disease transmission factors are increasingly understood, standard methods for preventing new infections improve.

Flavivirus

POWASSAN VIRUS, POW VIRUS

DESCRIPTION: The Powassan Virus is an RNA virus spread by ticks that feed on infected rodents. Most frequently, humans encounter the virus when bit by the blacklegged tick (*Ixodes scapularis*).

NATIVE DISTRIBUTION: It is endemic to North America and parts of Eurasia.

NORTH AMERICAN DISTRIBUTION: The Powassan Virus is found in Canada and the northeastern United States.

DATE(S) AND MEANS OF INTRODUCTION: It was first identified in 1958 in a child from Powassan, Ontario, Canada, who later died from the infection.

THREATS: Those infected may remain asymptomatic or develop a severe reaction leading to death. In extreme cases, brain swelling may occur, leading to meningitis. Up to half of all survivors may experience memory loss, headaches, and other long-term health concerns. Although still low, the incidence of infection is rising. As the global climate continues to change, new weather patterns of longer summers and warmer winters create more opportunities and time for ticks to acquire the pathogen from infected hosts and transmit the pathogen to humans. Global changes in weather patterns have also contributed to the expanded range of the blacklegged tick. These factors, plus the increase in the human population, all contribute to the increasing likelihood of exposure to infections like the Powassan Virus.

MANAGEMENT: There is no known treatment for the Powassan Virus, and infected individuals who experience severe disease are treated for symptoms. Infection can be prevented by avoiding tick bites.

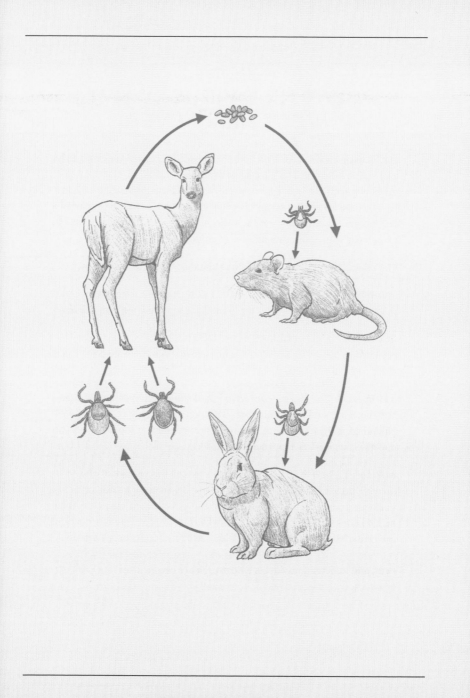

Flavivirus

WEST NILE VIRUS (WNV), WEST NILE FEVER

DESCRIPTION: The West Nile Virus is an RNA virus transmitted by mosquitoes that causes West Nile Fever in humans. It can also infect other vertebrates and can be especially fatal to birds. Symptoms of infection include fever, nausea, and headache. In severe cases, the symptoms last for weeks, and may result in permanent brain damage or death. 80 percent of infections result in no symptoms.

NATIVE DISTRIBUTION: It was first discovered in Uganda in 1937.

NORTH AMERICAN DISTRIBUTION: It can be found throughout most of North America, with thousands of cases reported every year.

DATE(S) AND MEANS OF INTRODUCTION: It was first reported in New York in 1999. It is not known how it arrived here, but it likely came in an infected bird or mosquito.

THREATS: The primary threat is the death of animals and humans, and the associated economic costs with prevention and treatment. West Nile Virus is the #1 cause of mosquito-borne illness in the United States and all U.S. cases are reported to the CDC.

MANAGEMENT: The best way to control the spread of the virus involves preventing mosquito bites, of which there are a myriad of tactics that can be employed by individuals and government agencies; these include city-wide spraying programs which are implemented throughout the United States to prevent WNV and other mosquito-borne disease.

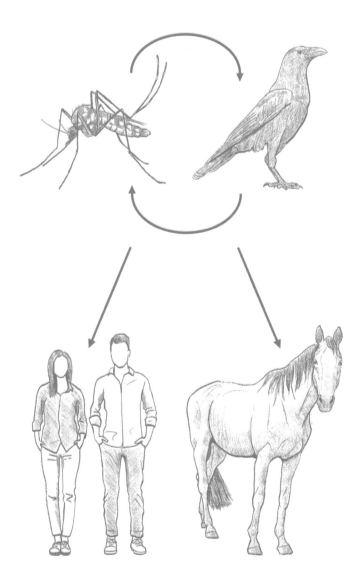

Mammarenavirus

LASSA VIRUS, LASSA, LASSA HEMORRHAGIC FEVER (LHF)

DESCRIPTION: Lassa is a zoonotic RNA virus that causes acute viral hemorrhagic fever. It is spread from the African rat (*Mastomys natalensis*) when humans ingest rat droppings or consume food exposed to rat urine.

NATIVE DISTRIBUTION: *Mammarenavirus* is endemic to Africa.

NORTH AMERICAN DISTRIBUTION: Seven cases have been reported in North America since 2010.

DATE(S) AND MEANS OF INTRODUCTION: In 1969, three American missionaries returning from West Africa brought the then unidentified virus back to North America. No human-to-human or animal-to-human transmission has occurred in North America.

THREATS: A majority (80 percent) of people who are exposed to Lassa Virus remain asymptomatic. About 20 percent of patients have a severe reaction, including hemorrhaging from the mouth and gut, and often require hospitalization. There is a 1 percent fatality rate in the general population, but very serious outcomes for pregnant people and fetuses. In late-stage pregnancy, infection can cause death in the mother or fetus about 80 percent of the time. Up to 20 percent of symptomatic people lose their hearing, although hearing does return in some individuals over time. About 300,000 to 500,000 people are infected each year, causing approximately 5,000 deaths. This is a pathogen of concern because it is predicted that global climate change will expand the range of the virus, causing a 600 percent increase in the number of individuals exposed to Lassa Virus.

MANAGEMENT: There is currently no effective vaccine, but the antiviral drug ribavirin is effectively used to treat some cases. Limiting human exposure to the African rat and maintaining hygienic conditions, including fastidiously covering food, can help reduce new infections. Human-to-human transmission is rare, but when it occurs is usually between patients and health-care workers. Humans may be infected and asymptomatic carriers. There is no screening for this disease in travelers, which does raise concerns for an increased likelihood of introducing the disease to new areas.

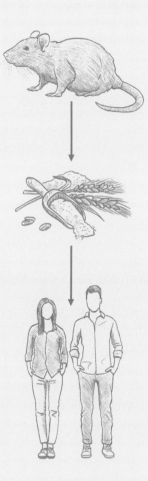

Orthoavulavirus

NEWCASTLE DISEASE VIRUS

DESCRIPTION: A highly contagious virus that infects birds. The virus infects both domestic and wild species. It spreads via respiration or ingestion of viral particles, so the virus can become especially prevalent where birds are kept in close proximity, such as a turkey farm, or in wild species that engage in flocking behavior. The severity of the disease depends on the viral strain and the host species, with common symptoms including weight loss, decreased egg production, malformed eggs, coughing, and neck twisting. The virus can spread throughout the bird's body, potentially leading to the animal's death.

NATIVE DISTRIBUTION: Native distribution is difficult to ascertain for the Newcastle Disease Virus, but it is currently considered endemic in many parts of the world.

NORTH AMERICAN DISTRIBUTION: In North America, it is present in parts of Mexico, the United States, and some Caribbean islands.

DATE(S) AND MEANS OF INTRODUCTION: It is believed that the first outbreak occurred during the 1920s in Southeast Asia, spreading worldwide over the next 30 years. A second outbreak occurred in the Middle East during the 1960s, taking only a decade to spread worldwide.

THREATS: It is one of the more deadly avian diseases because it has regular outbreaks and a high mortality rate. Control is challenging because it can infect many species. Mutations have created many viral strains. The virus can cause conjunctivitis in humans.

MANAGEMENT: Prevention of the disease is not unlike that for human viral infections: maintain good hygiene practices and use vaccinations.

Potyvirus

PLUM POX VIRUS

DESCRIPTION: A plant-pathogenic virus that primarily infects plants in the *Prunus* genus, which includes many important fruit-producing species, such as cherries, plums, and peaches. Symptoms of the Plum Pox Virus vary somewhat, depending on the host species, but usually include chlorosis and deformation of leaves and fruit.

NATIVE DISTRIBUTION: The native range is difficult to determine precisely, but the disease was first reported in Bulgaria in 1915, spreading throughout most of Europe over the next several decades.

NORTH AMERICAN DISTRIBUTION: It is currently only known to be present in Ontario, Canada. It has been detected in three U.S. states, but it has been considered eradicated in the United States since 2009.

DATE(S) AND MEANS OF INTRODUCTION: The disease was first detected in New York in 1999 and in Canada in 2000. The infection is vectored and transmitted by aphids and the transport of infected trees.

THREATS: Because the disease is not fatal to infected trees, the impact is primarily economical. During outbreaks, a significant portion of the fruits produced will be unpalatable, and fruit orchards may be destroyed to eliminate the virus.

MANAGEMENT: There is no direct control method that can be used on the Plum Pox Virus. Instead, efforts are focused on preventing its spread from its present location. Strategies to prevent the spread include the removal of diseased trees, applying insecticides to control the aphid vector, and other methods to control the aphid population. Additional efforts are underway to breed *Prunus* hybrids that are resistant to the virus.